The Basics of
READING TAROT

Your journey starts here.

Lisa Tjaden

Copyright © 2024 by Lisa Tjaden

Published by SideStreet Media
RadianceGifts.com

All rights reserved. No part of this publication may be reproduced, distributed, or transmitted in any form or by any means, including photocopying, recording, or other electronic or mechanical methods, without the prior written permission of the publisher, except in the case of brief quotations embodied in critical reviews and certain other noncommercial uses permitted by copyright law.

ISBN: 978-1-7750340-9-4

This book is dedicated to Seekers everywhere. May it serve as a resource to help on your journey to personal empowerment.

CONTENTS

Introduction — Page 9
What is Tarot?
Why Read Tarot?

Chapter 1: Understanding the Tarot Deck — Page 11
Structure of a Tarot Deck
The Major Arcana
The Minor Arcana

Chapter 2: The Language of Tarot — Page 15
Symbolism and Imagery
Numerology in Tarot
Astrology and Tarot

Chapter 3: Preparing for a Tarot Reading — Page 19
Choosing Your Tarot Deck
Cleansing and Connecting with Your Deck
Creating a Sacred Space

Chapter 4: How to Read Tarot Cards — Page 23
The Basics of a Tarot Reading
Reading Spreads
Intuitive Reading vs. Traditional Meanings

Chapter 5: Interpreting Tarot Cards — Page 29
Card Combinations
Reading Reversed Cards
Timing in Tarot

Chapter 6: Advanced Tarot Techniques — Page 33
Using Tarot for Self-Reflection
Tarot and Meditation
Tarot and Manifestation

Chapter 7: Tarot Ethics and Best Practices — Page 35
Ethical Considerations in Tarot
Reading for Others
Dealing with Difficult Readings

Chapter 8: Developing Your Tarot Skills — Page 37
Daily Tarot Practice
Expanding Your Knowledge
Creating Your Own Tarot Spreads

Major Arcana Cards — Page 41
- The Fool: 42
- The Magician: 42
- The High Priestess: 43
- The Empress: 43
- The Emperor: 44
- The Hierophant: 44
- The Lovers: 45
- The Chariot: 45
- Strength: 46
- The Hermit: 46
- Wheel of Fortune: 47
- Justice: 47
- The Hanged Man: 48
- Death: 48
- Temperance: 49
- The Devil: 49
- The Tower: 50
- The Star: 50
- The Moon: 51
- The Sun: 51
- Judgment: 52
- The World: 52

Minor Arcana — Page 53
- Pentacles: 54
- Cups: 61
- Swords: 68
- Wands: 75

Appendix - Glossary of Tarot Terms — Page 83

Introduction
The Basics of Reading Tarot

What is Tarot?
Tarot is a mystical and ancient practice that has captivated the human imagination for centuries. At its core, Tarot is a deck of 78 cards, each rich with symbolism, imagery, and meaning. These cards are not merely pieces of paper; they are tools for divination, self-reflection, and spiritual growth. Tarot can provide insights into our past, present, and future, helping us navigate life's challenges and opportunities with greater awareness.

A Brief History and Origin of Tarot
The origins of Tarot are shrouded in mystery, with roots tracing back to the late 14th or early 15th century in Europe. Initially, Tarot cards were used as playing cards, much like modern-day card games. However, by the 18th century, they had evolved into a powerful tool for divination and esoteric practices. The connection between Tarot and the mystical arts likely began in France, where occultists like Jean-Baptiste Alliette (known as Etteilla) popularized the use of Tarot for fortune-telling.

The Tarot deck is divided into two main parts: the Major Arcana and the Minor Arcana. The Major Arcana consists of 22 cards that represent significant life events, spiritual lessons, and karmic influences. These cards, such as The Fool, The Magician, and The High Priestess, are often seen as the most powerful and profound in a reading. The Minor Arcana, on the other hand, consists of 56 cards divided into four suits—Pentacles, Cups, Swords and Wands—each representing different aspects of life, from emotions and relationships to work and material concerns.

The Uses of Tarot in Divination, Self-Reflection, and Spiritual Growth

Over the centuries, Tarot has evolved into more than just a tool for predicting the future. It has become a powerful instrument for self-reflection and spiritual growth. Each card in the

Tarot deck carries its own unique energy and message, offering insights into our innermost thoughts, feelings, and desires. Through the practice of Tarot reading, we can gain clarity on our current situation, uncover hidden patterns in our behavior, and explore potential outcomes of our decisions.

In divination, Tarot is used to answer questions, providing guidance and foresight on various aspects of life. Whether you're seeking advice on love, career, or personal challenges, a Tarot reading can illuminate the path ahead and help you make informed choices.

Beyond divination, Tarot is also a powerful tool for self-reflection. By meditating on the images and symbols of the cards, we can connect with our subconscious mind and gain a deeper understanding of ourselves. Tarot encourages us to explore our inner world, confront our fears, and embrace our strengths. It's a mirror that reflects our true selves, helping us navigate the complexities of life with greater self-awareness.

Finally, Tarot is a means of spiritual growth. Many people use Tarot as a part of their spiritual practice, integrating it into rituals, meditation, and journaling. The cards serve as a bridge between the conscious and the divine, offering insights and wisdom from higher realms. Whether you're seeking to connect with your higher self, spirit guides, or the universe, Tarot can be a profound tool for spiritual exploration.

Tarot as a Tool for Personal Development

Tarot is not about predicting the future; it's about shaping it. By using Tarot as a tool for personal development, you can set intentions, manifest your desires, and create the life you want. The cards can help you identify your goals, overcome obstacles, and stay aligned with your true purpose. They can also provide the motivation and inspiration needed to pursue your dreams with confidence and clarity.

Chapter 1: Understanding the Tarot Deck

Tarot has long been a source of fascination and mystery, with its rich symbolism and profound insights into the human experience. To fully harness the power of Tarot, it is essential to understand the structure and components of the Tarot deck. In this chapter, we will explore the two main sections of the Tarot deck: the Major Arcana and the Minor Arcana. We will also delve into the four suits of the Minor Arcana—Pentacles, Cups, Swords, and Wands—and examine their symbolic meanings and significance in readings.

Structure of a Tarot Deck

A standard Tarot deck consists of 78 cards, divided into two main sections: the Major Arcana and the Minor Arcana. Each section serves a distinct purpose and carries its own unique energy and symbolism.

The Major Arcana

The Major Arcana is composed of 22 cards, numbered from 0 to 21. These cards represent significant life events, spiritual lessons, and karmic influences that shape our journey. The Major Arcana is often considered the heart of the Tarot deck, as it reflects the overarching themes and energies that guide our lives.

Each card in the Major Arcana has a specific name and imagery that conveys its meaning. For example, "The Fool," numbered 0, represents new beginnings, innocence, and spontaneity, while "The World," numbered 21, symbolizes completion, fulfillment, and achievement. The cards of the Major Arcana are often seen as the "big picture" aspects of a Tarot reading, revealing the larger forces at play in a person's life.

The Minor Arcana

The Minor Arcana consists of 56 cards, divided into four suits: Pentacles, Cups, Swords and Wands. Each suit contains 14 cards, including 10 numbered cards (Ace through Ten) and four Court Cards (Page, Knight, Queen, and King).

While the Major Arcana focuses on broader spiritual and existential themes, the Minor Arcana deals with the everyday experiences and situations that we encounter in our lives. Each suit represents a different aspect of life and carries its own symbolic meaning

The Major Arcana

The 22 cards of the Major Arcana are the most powerful and significant in a Tarot reading. Each card tells a story, representing different stages in the journey of life, known as "The Fool's Journey." This journey begins with the innocence and potential of "The Fool" and culminates in the completeness and wisdom of "The World."

Here is a brief overview of some of the Major Arcana cards and their meanings:
- **The Fool** (0): Represents new beginnings, innocence, and taking a leap of faith.
- **The Magician** (1): Symbolizes willpower, creativity, and manifestation.
- **The High Priestess** (2): Represents intuition, mystery, and the subconscious mind.
- **The Empress** (3): Symbolizes fertility, abundance, and nurturing energy.
- **The Emperor** (4): Represents authority, structure, and control.
- **The Hierophant** (5): Symbolizes tradition, spiritual guidance, and conformity.
- **The Lovers** (6): Represents love, relationships, and choices.
- **The Chariot** (7): Symbolizes determination, control, and victory.
- **Strength** (8): Represents inner strength, courage, and patience.
- **The Hermit** (9): Symbolizes introspection, solitude, and inner wisdom.
- **Wheel of Fortune** (10): Represents fate, cycles, and change.
- **Justice** (11): Symbolizes fairness, balance, and legal matters.
- **The Hanged Man** (12): Represents surrender, perspective, and letting go.
- **Death** (13): Symbolizes transformation, endings, and new beginnings.
- **Temperance** (14): Represents balance, moderation, and harmony.
- **The Devil** (15): Symbolizes materialism, temptation, and bondage.
- **The Tower** (16): Represents sudden change, upheaval, and revelation.
- **The Star** (17): Symbolizes hope, inspiration, and personal power.
- **The Moon** (18): Represents illusion, intuition, and the subconscious.
- **The Sun** (19): Symbolizes success, vitality, and joy.
- **Judgement** (20): Represents rebirth, evaluation, and awakening.
- **The World** (21): Symbolizes completion and fulfillment.

The Minor Arcana

The Minor Arcana cards provide insight into the more specific and day-to-day aspects of life. Each suit in the Minor Arcana represents different themes and areas of life, and the cards within each suit convey a range of emotions and experiences.

The Four Suits

Pentacles: The suit of Pentacles is associated with the element of earth and symbolizes material wealth, career, health, and the physical world. Pentacles are typically seen in readings about finances, work, medical concerns and practical matters. Pentacles focus on the material world, including finances, work, and physical health. The Ace of Pentacles symbolizes new opportunities for prosperity, while the Ten of Pentacles represents wealth, legacy, and the culmination of hard work.

Cups: The suit of Cups is connected to the element of water and symbolizes emotions, relationships, and the subconscious. Cups are commonly seen in readings about love and emotional well-being. Cups are the suit of emotions and relationships, representing the heart and the soul. The Ace of Cups often signifies the beginning of a new relationship or emotional experience, while the Ten of Cups reflects a sense of fulfillment and happiness in relationships.

Swords: The suit of Swords is linked to the element of air and represents intellect, communication, conflict, and decision-making. Swords often appear in readings concerning challenges, conflicts, and mental clarity. Swords deal with the mind and intellect, often highlighting conflicts, challenges, and decisions. The Ace of Swords represents mental clarity and the power of thought, while the Ten of Swords may indicate a painful ending or a moment of profound realization.

Wands: The suit of Wands is associated with the element of fire and represents creativity, action, passion, and ambition. Wands often appear in readings related to intuition, morals, beliefs and personal growth. As the suit of creativity and action, Wands represent our passions, ambitions, and the energy we put into our endeavors. The Ace of Wands, for example, symbolizes the spark of a new idea or project, while the Ten of Wands may indicate the burden of too many responsibilities.

Numbered Cards (Ace through Ten)

The numbered cards in each suit follow a progression from the beginning of a journey (Ace) to its completion (Ten). Each card in this sequence represents a different stage of growth and development:

- **Ace:** Represents new beginnings and potential.
- **Two:** Indicates balance, partnership, and choices.
- **Three:** Symbolizes growth, collaboration, and creativity.
- **Four:** Represents stability, security, and foundations.
- **Five:** Reflects inner conflict, change, and challenge.

- **Six:** Indicates harmony, resolution, and progress.
- **Seven:** Represents reflection, external challenges, and perseverance.
- **Eight:** Symbolizes movement, action, and progress.
- **Nine:** Indicates fulfillment, independence, and contentment.
- **Ten:** Represents completion, culmination, and legacy.

Threes, Sixes and Nines mark a level of completion in that suit, before moving to the next level of growth.

Court Cards (Page, Knight, Queen, and King)

The Court Cards are the "personalities" of the Tarot deck, representing different aspects of human character and behavior. Each Court Card can represent an actual person in your life, a role you are playing, or an aspect of your own personality:

Page: Represents youth, curiosity, and the beginning of a new phase.
Knight: Symbolizes action, movement, and the pursuit of goals.
Queen: Represents nurturing, maturity, and emotional depth. Introspection.
King: Symbolizes authority, leadership, and mastery. Extroversion.

Understanding the structure of the Tarot deck is essential for any aspiring Tarot reader. Each card, whether part of the Major or Minor Arcana, carries its own unique energy and message. By familiarizing yourself with the different suits, numbered cards, and Court Cards, you can begin to unlock the deeper meanings of the Tarot and use it as a powerful tool for insight, guidance, and personal growth. By fully understanding the basic formula of Tarot, you are able to interpret the cards, rather than memorizing them individually.

Chapter 2:
The Language of Tarot

The Tarot is a rich tapestry of symbols, imagery, and esoteric connections that, when understood, can offer profound insights into your life's journey. In this chapter, we will explore the language of Tarot, focusing on the symbolism and imagery found within the cards, the role of numerology in Tarot, and the connections between Tarot and astrology. Understanding these elements will enhance your ability to interpret the cards and unlock their deeper meanings.

Symbolism and Imagery

Tarot cards are filled with intricate symbols and imagery that carry deep meaning. Each element on a card—whether it's a figure, an object, a color, or an animal—contributes to the card's overall message. Learning to interpret these symbols is key to understanding the Tarot's language.

The Fool's Journey

One of the most significant symbolic narratives within the Tarot is "The Fool's Journey." The Fool, represented by the card numbered 0, embarks on a journey through the Major Arcana, encountering various archetypes along the way. This journey symbolizes the soul's path to enlightenment, with each card representing a stage of growth and learning.

For example, when the Fool meets The Magician (card 1), he encounters the power of manifestation and personal will. As he progresses to The High Priestess (card 2), he learns about intuition and the mysteries of the subconscious. This journey through the Major Arcana is a metaphor for the spiritual evolution that we all undergo in life.

Elemental Associations

The four suits of the Minor Arcana—Pentacles, Cups, Swords and Wands—are each associated with one of the four classical elements: fire, water, air, and earth, respectively.

These elements influence the nature of the cards within each suit:
- **Pentacles** (Earth): Symbolizes material wealth, physical health, stability, and the tangible aspects of life. Earth is grounding and practical, concerned with the physical world and security.
- **Cups** (Water): Symbolizes emotions, relationships, and the subconscious. Water is fluid and adaptable, reflecting the ebb and flow of feelings and emotional connections.
- **Swords** (Air): Represents intellect, communication, conflict, and decision-making. Air is associated with the mind, thoughts, and the challenges that come with mental clarity and conflict resolution.
- **Wands** (Fire): Represents energy, passion, creativity, and action. Fire is dynamic and transformative, often symbolizing ambition and drive.

Colors and Animals

Colors in Tarot cards are not random; they carry specific meanings that can influence a card's interpretation:
- **Red:** Represents passion, energy, and action.
- **Blue:** Symbolizes calm, intuition, and spirituality.
- **Yellow:** Reflects optimism, clarity, and intellectual energy.
- **Green:** Represents growth, abundance, and healing.

Animals depicted in Tarot cards also have symbolic meanings. For instance, the dog that accompanies The Fool represents loyalty and protection, while the lion in the Strength card symbolizes courage, inner strength, and primal instincts.

Numerology in Tarot

Numerology is the study of the esoteric significance of numbers and plays an important role in Tarot. Each card's number carries a specific vibration and meaning that influences the card's interpretation.

The Meanings of Numbers in Tarot
- **One** (Ace): Represents beginnings, potential, and unity. Aces are the seeds of possibility in the Tarot, symbolizing new opportunities and the essence of their suit.
- **Two:** Symbolizes balance, duality, partnerships, and choices. Twos often represent the need to make a decision or bring harmony to opposing forces.
- **Three:** Represents creativity, growth, and expansion. Threes often signify the results of a partnership or collaboration.

- **Four:** Symbolizes stability, structure, and foundation. Fours represent solid foundations and the need for order and organization.
- **Five:** Represents conflict, change, and instability. Fives often signal challenges and the need for adaptation and flexibility.
- **Six:** Symbolizes harmony, resolution, and balance. Sixes often represent a return to harmony after a period of struggle or imbalance.
- **Seven:** Represents introspection, spiritual development, and assessment. Sevens often encourage reflection and deeper understanding.
- **Eight:** Symbolizes strength, power, and progress. Eights represent movement, advancement, and the manifestation of goals.
- **Nine:** Represents fulfillment, completion, and reflection. Nines signal the near end of a cycle and the need to review and reflect.
- **Ten:** Symbolizes completion, culmination, and transformation. Tens represent the end of a cycle and the potential for a new beginning.

Numerology adds another layer of depth to Tarot readings, allowing you to interpret the significance of numbers in conjunction with the card's imagery and symbolism.

Astrology and Tarot

Astrology and Tarot are closely linked, with many Tarot cards being associated with specific astrological signs and planets. This connection adds a cosmic dimension to Tarot readings, providing insight into how celestial influences might be affecting the situation at hand.

Astrological Signs and Tarot Cards

Each of the 12 astrological signs is associated with a particular Tarot card:

- **Aries:** The Emperor (Card 4) - Represents leadership, authority, and assertiveness.
- **Taurus:** The Hierophant (Card 5) - Symbolizes tradition, stability, and spiritual guidance.
- **Gemini:** The Lovers (Card 6) - Represents choices, communication, and duality.
- **Cancer:** The Chariot (Card 7) - Symbolizes determination, willpower, and emotional balance.
- **Leo:** Strength (Card 8) - Represents courage, inner strength, and self-confidence.
- **Virgo:** The Hermit (Card 9) - Symbolizes introspection, wisdom, and solitude.
- **Libra:** Justice (Card 11) - Represents fairness, balance, and legal matters.
- **Scorpio:** Death (Card 13) - Symbolizes transformation, endings, and new beginnings.
- **Sagittarius:** Temperance (Card 14) - Represents balance, moderation, and harmony.
- **Capricorn:** The Devil (Card 15) - Symbolizes materialism, temptation, and bondage.

- **Aquarius:** The Star (Card 17) - Represents hope, inspiration, and spiritual insight.
- **Pisces:** The Moon (Card 18) - Symbolizes intuition, dreams, and the subconscious.

Planets and Tarot Cards

In addition to astrological signs, certain Tarot cards are also associated with planets:

- **The Magician** (Mercury): Represents communication, intellect, and skill.
- **The High Priestess** (Moon): Symbolizes intuition, mystery, and the subconscious.
- **The Empress** (Venus): Represents love, beauty, and abundance.
- **The Tower** (Mars): Symbolizes sudden change, upheaval, and destruction.
- **The Sun** (Sun): Represents vitality, success, and joy.

These astrological associations can deepen your understanding of a Tarot card's meaning, especially when considering how planetary influences might be affecting the querent's situation.

The language of Tarot is rich with symbolism, numerology, and astrological connections. By understanding and interpreting these elements, you can unlock the deeper meanings of the cards and gain greater insight into your readings. Whether you're interpreting the colors and symbols in a card, exploring the numerological significance, or considering the astrological influences, each element contributes to the story that the Tarot is telling.

Chapter 3:
Preparing for a Tarot Reading

Preparing for a Tarot reading involves more than just shuffling and drawing cards. It's about creating a connection with your deck, setting the right environment, and ensuring your mind and spirit are ready to receive the insights the cards have to offer. This chapter will guide you through the essential steps of choosing your Tarot deck, cleansing and connecting with it, and creating a sacred space for your readings.

Choosing Your Tarot Deck

The first step in your Tarot journey is choosing a deck that resonates with you. With so many options available, it can be overwhelming to decide on the right one. Here are some tips to help you make your choice:

- **Resonance and Intuition:** Your Tarot deck should feel like an extension of yourself. When you look at the images, they should speak to you on an intuitive level. You may feel more comfortable with a deck that expresses your personal life choices or hobbies and interests. Trust your gut feeling—if a deck draws you in or feels right in your hands, it's likely the one for you.
- **Artwork and Symbolism:** Different decks feature various artistic styles and symbolic interpretations. Some decks, like the Rider-Waite-Smith, are rich in traditional symbolism, while others, like the Thoth Tarot, offer more esoteric and abstract imagery. Consider what type of artwork and symbolism you feel most connected to, as this will impact your readings. For a beginner, it is often helpful to choose a deck that is clearly numbered or illustrated. (3 coins on the 3 of Pentacles)

- **Purpose and Use:** Consider what you intend to use the Tarot for. Some decks are better suited for self-reflection and meditation, while others are more geared towards divination and predictive readings. For beginners, the Rider-Waite-Smith deck is often recommended due to its straightforward symbolism and wide availability of learning resources.

Popular Decks: Some of the most popular Tarot decks include:
  - **Rider-Waite-Smith:** Known for its accessible symbolism and clear imagery, it is one of the most widely used decks.
  - **Thoth Tarot:** Created by Aleister Crowley and Lady Frieda Harris, this deck is known for its rich, esoteric symbolism and powerful imagery.
  - **The Wild Unknown Tarot:** Popular for its minimalist, nature-inspired artwork, this deck appeals to those seeking a connection to Earth.
  - **Angel Tarot:** I recommend all of Radleigh Valentine's decks, especially for new readers as each card has a description printed on it. This simplifies interpretation and helps to familiarize you to Tarot.

Choosing your Tarot deck is a personal decision, and there is no right or wrong choice. The most important thing is that the deck you select feels right to you and inspires a sense of curiosity and connection.

Cleansing and Connecting with Your Deck

Once you've chosen your Tarot deck, the next step is to cleanse and connect with it. This process helps to remove any lingering energies from the deck's previous environments and allows you to establish a personal bond with your cards.

Cleansing Your Deck

There are several methods for cleansing your Tarot deck, and you can choose the one that resonates most with you:

- **Crystals:** Place a clear quartz or selenite crystal on top of your deck to cleanse it. These crystals are known for their purifying properties and can help clear away any unwanted energy.
- **Moonlight:** Leave your deck under the light of the full moon to recharge and purify it. The moon's energy is gentle and nurturing, making it an excellent way to cleanse your deck.
- **Smudging:** Use sage, palo santo, or another cleansing herb to smudge your deck. Simply pass the deck through the smoke, allowing it to absorb the purifying energy.
- **Salt:** Bury your deck in a bowl of salt overnight. Salt is known for its ability to absorb negative energies. Be sure to use fine, non-iodized salt, and place your deck in a protective cloth before burying it. Do not reuse this salt in cooking or bathing. Dispose of it.

The simplest cleansing technique is to knock three times on your deck before shuffling.

Connecting with Your Deck

After cleansing, it's important to establish a personal connection with your deck. This connection will deepen your readings and help you develop your intuitive abilities:

- **Meditate with Your Deck:** Spend time holding your deck in your hands while meditating. Visualize a connection between you and the cards, allowing your energy to merge with theirs.
- **Study the Imagery:** Take the time to go through each card, one by one. Observe the imagery, symbols, and colors, and take note of any emotions or thoughts that arise. This will help you become more familiar with the deck and its unique language.
- **Sleep with Your Deck:** Place your deck under your pillow or on your bedside table for a few nights. This helps to infuse the cards with your energy and establish a strong connection between you and the deck.
- **Daily Draws:** Incorporate your Tarot deck into your daily routine by drawing a card each morning. This practice not only helps you connect with your deck but also allows you to develop a daily dialogue with the cards.

Creating a Sacred Space

The environment in which you conduct your Tarot readings plays a significant role in the quality and clarity of your readings. Creating a sacred space helps to focus your mind, set the right intentions, and ensure that you are grounded and centered before drawing the cards.

Setting Up Your Space

Your sacred space can be anywhere that feels peaceful and private to you. Whether it's a dedicated altar, a cozy corner of your room, or even a spot outside in nature, the key is to create an environment that promotes calm and focus:

- **Choose a Quiet Space:** Find a location where you won't be disturbed. A quiet space helps you to tune in to your intuition and the messages from the Tarot.
- **Cleanse the Area:** Just as you cleanse your deck, it's important to cleanse your reading space. You can use smudging, crystals, or simply your intention to clear any negative or stagnant energy from the area.
- **Set the Mood:** Lighting a candle, burning incense, or playing soft music can help create a relaxing atmosphere. These elements can also serve as a signal to your mind that you are entering a sacred and focused space. This prepares you and indicates to your guides that you are paying attention.

Ritual and Intention-Setting

Rituals and intention-setting are powerful tools that can enhance your Tarot readings. They help to ground your energy, focus your mind, and align your intentions with the guidance you seek:

- **Grounding:** Before you begin your reading, take a moment to ground yourself. This can be done through deep breathing, visualization, or a simple grounding exercise like imagining roots growing from your feet into the earth. I find that gently tapping my thymus gland (located in the little space at the top of your breastbone) for 10-15 seconds is an excellent way to ground myself.
- **Set Your Intention:** Clearly state your intention for the reading. This could be a question you want answered, guidance on a particular issue, or simply a desire to connect with your higher self. Setting an intention helps to focus the reading and align the cards with your purpose. At this point I add a prayer or invocation. I greet my guides and ask them to join me in the reading. I ask for my ears, heart and consciousness to be open to the answers. Always finish any invocation or prayer with an expression of gratitude.
- **Shuffle with Purpose:** As you shuffle your deck, keep your intention in mind. This not only helps to clear your mind of distractions but also infuses the deck with your question or focus for the reading.

Preparing for a Tarot reading is an essential part of the Tarot practice. By choosing a deck that resonates with you, cleansing and connecting with it, and creating a sacred space for your readings, you lay the foundation for insightful and meaningful Tarot experiences. These steps help to ensure that you are fully present, focused, and open to the guidance that the Tarot has to offer.

Chapter 4:
How to Read Tarot Cards

Reading Tarot cards is both an art and a practice, combining intuition with traditional knowledge. Whether you're seeking insight into a specific situation or exploring the cards for personal growth, understanding how to approach a Tarot reading is essential. In this chapter, we'll explore the basics of a Tarot reading, different Tarot spreads, and the balance between intuitive and traditional interpretations.

The Basics of a Tarot Reading

Performing a Tarot reading involves a few fundamental steps that help to ground the reading and focus the energies of the cards. Here's a step-by-step guide to get you started:

1. Set Your Intention

Before you begin, take a moment to set your intention for the reading. This could be a specific question you want to explore, or a general request for guidance. Setting an intention helps to focus your mind and directs the energy of the reading towards a clear purpose.

2. Shuffling the Cards

Shuffling the deck is a crucial step in any Tarot reading. As you shuffle, concentrate on your intention or question. This helps to infuse the deck with your energy and aligns the cards with your inquiry. There are no strict rules on how to shuffle; you can use the traditional overhand shuffle, riffle shuffle, or simply mix the cards on the tabletop. Some people are opposed to the riffle shuffle, feeling that it is disrespectful to the cards. Since the intention is to put your energy into the cards it is my belief that you use whatever is most comfortable for you.

3. Cutting the Deck After shuffling, you can cut the deck to finalize the mixing process. You might choose to cut the deck into three piles and then reassemble them, or you can ask the querent (the person for whom you're reading) to cut the deck. This step further personalize the reading. I always cut the deck with my left hand into three piles. I draw the middle pile first, place it on top of the left hand pile and then pick up the last pile. The top card is then the beginning of your reading.

4. Drawing the Cards Once the deck is shuffled and cut, it's time to draw the cards. The number of cards you draw depends on the spread you're using (more on spreads below). As you draw each card, lay them out in the positions dictated by the spread you've chosen.

5. Interpreting the Cards With the cards laid out, begin interpreting their meanings. Look at the imagery, symbolism, and position of each card in the spread. Consider how the cards relate to one another and how they answer the question or intention you set at the beginning of the reading.

Reading Spreads

A Tarot spread is the layout of the cards in a reading. Each position in a spread has a specific meaning that influences the interpretation of the card placed in it. Here are some popular Tarot spreads and how to use them:

1. One-Card Spread For a quick and focused answer, the One-Card Spread is a go-to option. This spread involves drawing just one card to provide insight or guidance on a specific issue. It's perfect for daily draws, quick checks, or when you need a clear and direct answer.

2. Three-Card Spread The Three-Card Spread is a simple yet powerful layout that can be used for various types of questions. The three cards typically represent:

- **Past:** The first card reflects the past influences on the situation.
- **Present:** The second card represents the current state of affairs.
- **Outcome:** The third card indicates the likely outcome or future developments.

This spread is ideal for beginners and provides a concise snapshot of a situation.

Past

Present

Future

3. Celtic Cross Spread The Celtic Cross is one of the most popular and comprehensive Tarot spreads. You will find a picture of the layout for this spread below. It consists of ten cards, each representing different aspects of the querent's life or question:

- **Card 1:** The present situation.
- **Card 2:** The challenge or obstacle. This card can also act as a bridge supporting the situation
- **Card 3:** The Free Will Card (or how you can choose to react to the situation)
- **Card 4:** Root Cause or Distant Past. Sometimes ancestors or past lives can come into play here.
- **Card 5:** Recent Past (yesterday and up to one year ago usually)
- **Card 6:** The Present
- **Card 7:** The Qualities you bring to bear regarding the situation
- **Card 8:** The Environment you find yourself in regarding the situation.
- **Card 9:** Hopes and fears.
- **Card 10:** The Outcome. Remember this is never set in stone. You have free will so the outcome can always be changed by choices you make moving forward.

The Celtic Cross offers a deep and detailed reading, making it suitable for complex questions or when a thorough exploration is needed.

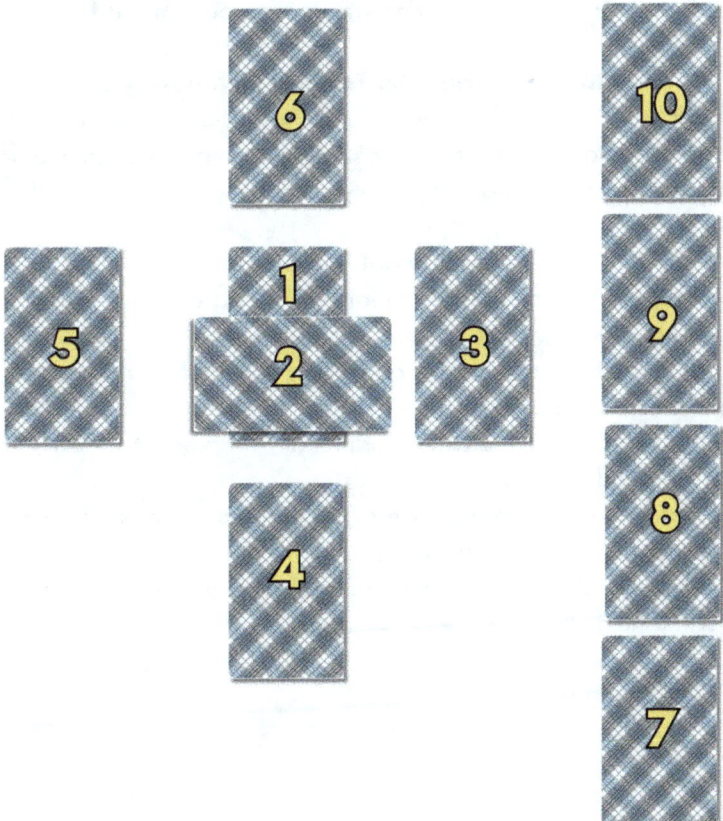

4. Other Spreads

There are countless other spreads tailored to specific types of questions or areas of life, such as relationship spreads, career spreads, and chakra spreads. As you become more comfortable with reading Tarot, you may even create your own custom spreads that align with your personal style and needs. A fun tarot exercise is to discover your soul card. This helps you to understand your motivations and purpose in this lifetime. It is determined by adding the numbers of your birth (day, month and year) and finding the corresponding card in the major arcana.

Birthday: June 29, 1967

Add: 06
29
+ 1967
2002
2 + 0 + 0 + 2 = 4
Emperor Card

Some of you will have more than one number, like 19 which distills down to 10 (1+9) and then 1 (1+0). Examine the meaning of all of those cards in the major arcana. I'm sure you will find that they reflect your soul. This technique also works if you substitute the current year to determine your soul path at this time.

Intuitive Reading vs. Traditional Meanings

One of the most profound aspects of Tarot reading is the balance between intuition and traditional card meanings. Both approaches are valuable, and learning to harmonize them can enhance your readings.

Traditional Meanings

Each Tarot card has established meanings based on its symbolism, imagery, and placement within the Tarot deck. These meanings have been passed down through centuries of Tarot practice and are often rooted in historical, cultural, and esoteric traditions. For example:

- **The Fool (Major Arcana):** Traditionally represents new beginnings, spontaneity, and taking a leap of faith.
- **The Ten of Swords (Minor Arcana):** Symbolizes endings, betrayal, and loss, but also the possibility of a new dawn.

Familiarizing yourself with the traditional meanings provides a solid foundation for interpreting the cards.

Intuitive Reading

Intuitive reading involves trusting your gut feelings and personal insights when interpreting the cards. This approach allows you to go beyond the traditional meanings and tap into the unique energy of the reading. You might notice certain colors, symbols, or emotions that stand out to you, and these intuitive hits can offer deeper layers of meaning.

- **For example:** You might draw The Fool and, instead of focusing on its traditional meaning, you might be drawn to the cliff the figure is about to step off, interpreting it as a warning to look before you leap.

Developing confidence in your intuition takes practice, but over time, you'll find that your personal insights add richness and depth to your readings.

Balancing the Two

The best Tarot readings often blend traditional meanings with intuitive insights. Start by considering the traditional interpretation of a card, then allow your intuition to guide you in understanding how that meaning applies to the specific context of your reading. Over time, you'll develop a personal style that integrates both approaches, making your readings more accurate and resonant. Keep an open mind! Your interpretation of individual cards will change with your different life experiences.

Learning how to read Tarot cards is a journey of both study and self-discovery. By understanding the basics of a Tarot reading, familiarizing yourself with different spreads, and finding the balance between traditional meanings and intuitive insights, you'll be well on your way to providing meaningful and accurate readings. In the next chapter, we will explore how to interpret specific card combinations and how to weave together the story told by the cards in a reading.

Chapter 5: Interpreting Tarot Cards

Interpreting Tarot cards is both an art and a skill that evolves with practice. Each card carries its own meaning, but when combined with others, their interaction can reveal deeper insights and more complex narratives. In this chapter, we'll explore how to interpret card combinations, understand reversed cards, and determine timing within a reading.

Card Combinations

Tarot readings rarely involve a single card in isolation. Instead, the true depth of a reading comes from how multiple cards interact with one another. Understanding these interactions can unlock a richer interpretation of the message being conveyed.

1. The Interplay of Cards

When reading Tarot, consider how cards influence each other. For instance, the presence of a Major Arcana card often signifies a significant life event, while the Minor Arcana provides context or details surrounding that event. A Major Arcana card like The Lovers appearing alongside a card like the Two of Cups can emphasize themes of partnership and love, perhaps indicating a deep, soul-level connection. Also consider the balance of Major vs Minor in your spread. In a 10 card spread one could expect 2-3 of the cards to be Major Arcana, as they make up roughly 28% of the deck. If that number is higher than that it indicates that the reading is of more significance to the "Big Picture" rather than day to day life.

As we discussed earlier, the Minor Arcana cards represent the beginning to the completion in each individual suit. If the spread is made up of lower vibration cards (1-5) as opposed to higher vibration cards (6-10) that indicates that growth is necessary regarding the situation.

I also consider the balance of suits in a spread. If there is a large number of cups and lack of swords it could indicate that you are approaching the situation emotionally rather than logically. I say that your Kirks are battling your Spocks!

2. Supporting and Contradictory Cards

Look for cards that either support or contradict each other. For example, if you draw The Sun (a card of joy and success) alongside the Ten of Swords (a card of endings and betrayal), the reading may indicate that even after a painful ending, a positive new beginning is on the horizon. Conversely, if you draw The Chariot (indicating forward movement) with the Eight of Swords (indicating feeling trapped), it might suggest that while you have the potential to move forward, something is holding you back.

3. Elemental Dignities

Another method of interpreting card combinations is through elemental dignities. Each suit in the Minor Arcana is associated with an element—Pentacles (Earth), Cups (Water), Swords (Air) and Wands (Fire). Cards of the same element generally support each other, while opposing elements can create tension. For example, Fire (Wands) and Water (Cups) can clash, potentially indicating conflicting emotions and actions.

Reading Reversed Cards

Reversed cards, or cards that appear upside-down in a reading, add another layer of complexity. Some readers choose to include reversed cards, while others prefer to work exclusively with upright cards. If you decide to use reversals, understanding their significance is essential.

1. Common Approaches to Reversals

Reversed cards can be interpreted in several ways:

- **Opposite Meaning:** A reversed card might indicate the opposite of its upright meaning. For example, The Star, typically representing hope and inspiration, might suggest a lack of faith or pessimism when reversed.
- **Blocked Energy:** Reversals can also signify blocked or delayed energy. For example, The Wheel of Fortune reversed might indicate a period of stagnation or resistance to change.
- **Internalization:** Some readers see reversals as representing internal experiences rather than external events. For instance, The Hermit reversed could suggest a period of deep inner reflection rather than outward solitude.

2. Deciding Whether to Use Reversals

Whether to use reversals is a personal choice. Some readers feel that reversals provide a fuller picture, while others find that they complicate the reading unnecessarily. If you're a beginner, you might start with upright cards only, gradually incorporating reversals as you become more comfortable.

Timing in Tarot

One of the most challenging aspects of Tarot reading is interpreting timing. While Tarot is primarily a tool for exploring possibilities rather than predicting exact outcomes, there are techniques you can use to gain insights into when events might unfold.

1. Card Positions and Timing

In certain spreads, specific card positions are associated with timeframes. For example, in a Celtic Cross spread, the "Recent Past" position typically refers to events that have occurred in the last few weeks to months. The "Outcome" position might point to a longer-term future, such as six months to a year.

2. Suits and Timing

Each suit in the Tarot deck is traditionally associated with a season or time period:

- **Pentacles** (Earth): Years or Winter.
- **Cups** (Water): Weeks or Autumn.
- **Swords** (Air): Months or Spring.
- **Wands** (Fire): Days or Summer.

These associations can be used to estimate when an event might take place. For instance, if a reading suggests that something will happen when the Ace of Cups appears, you might interpret this as occurring in the next few weeks or during the autumn season. Since this card is often associated with a new birth of a child, that could prove interesting.

3. Numerology and Timing

Numerology can also play a role in timing. Each number in the Tarot corresponds to a different phase or cycle. For example, Aces represent beginnings, while Tens indicate completion. If you draw a Four of Wands, it might suggest that something will happen in four days, weeks, or even during a period of celebration (like a holiday or anniversary).

Interpreting Tarot cards is an evolving process that deepens as you become more familiar with the cards and their interactions. By understanding how to interpret card combinations, using or choosing not to use reversed cards, and exploring techniques for timing, you'll develop a more nuanced and insightful approach to Tarot readings. In the next chapter, we'll delve into how to formulate effective questions for Tarot readings and how to interpret different types of queries, from simple yes/no questions to more complex inquiries about life and love.

Chapter 6: Advanced Tarot Techniques

Using Tarot for Self-Reflection

Tarot is more than just a tool for divination; it's a powerful mirror reflecting the inner workings of your mind and soul. By engaging with the cards on a deeper level, you can embark on a journey of self-discovery and personal growth.

Journaling with Tarot: One effective method of self-reflection through Tarot is journaling. After pulling a card, spend time writing about the emotions, thoughts, and memories it evokes. Ask yourself questions such as:

- How does this card relate to my current life situation?
- What message is it trying to convey about my personal growth?
- What action steps can I take based on this card's guidance?

Over time, these journal entries become a personal narrative that tracks your spiritual journey, providing insights that are often overlooked in daily life.

Meditating with Tarot: Meditation with Tarot is another profound way to deepen your connection with the cards and yourself. Select a card that resonates with your current state or question. Focus on the imagery, symbols, and emotions it stirs within you. As you close your eyes, visualize stepping into the card. What do you see, feel, or hear? Who or what do you encounter? Allow the card to guide you through a meditation that can reveal hidden aspects of yourself, offering clarity and wisdom.

By integrating Tarot into your meditation practice, you can tap into deeper subconscious messages, allowing for a more profound connection to your inner wisdom.

Tarot and Manifestation

Tarot is not only a reflective tool but also a creative one. It can be used to set intentions and manifest desires by aligning your energy with the cards.

Manifestation Techniques: To use Tarot in manifestation, begin by clearly defining your goal or desire. Choose cards that represent your intentions—The Magician for willpower, The Empress for abundance, or The Sun for success. Create a Tarot spread that outlines the steps needed to achieve your goal. For example, draw a card for each of the following:

- What is the first action I should take?
- What challenges might I face, and how can I overcome them?
- What will be the outcome if I follow this path?

After drawing the cards, meditate on them daily, visualize the outcome, and take action aligned with the guidance you receive. Tarot helps keep your intentions focused and your actions purposeful, aiding in the manifestation of your desires.

By exploring these advanced Tarot techniques, you can deepen your practice, using the cards not only for divination but as a versatile tool for personal growth, spiritual connection, and manifestation. The Tarot becomes a companion on your life journey, guiding you toward a more fulfilled and enlightened existence.

Chapter 7:
Tarot Ethics and Best Practices

Ethical Considerations in Tarot
1. **Respect Boundaries:** As a Tarot reader, it's crucial to respect the personal boundaries of your querents. Before conducting a reading, obtain clear consent and ensure that the querent is comfortable with the process. Avoid reading for someone without their explicit permission, and be mindful of sensitive topics. Do not offer advice that you are not qualified to give. Rather encourage the querent to seek out a professional.
2. **Maintain Confidentiality:** Confidentiality is a cornerstone of ethical Tarot practice. All personal information shared during a reading should remain private. This respect for privacy helps build trust and ensures that querents feel safe disclosing their concerns.
3. **Honor Free Will:** Tarot readings should empower rather than dictate. While the cards provide insights and guidance, the querent's free will is paramount. Emphasize that the future is not set in stone and that the cards offer possibilities rather than certainties. Encourage querents to use the insights gained to make informed decisions rather than feeling pressured by the reading.

Reading for Others
Tips for Reading Tarot for Friends, Family, and Clients
   Maintain Professionalism: Even when reading for friends or family, approach the reading with the same level of professionalism you would with a stranger.

This helps maintain the integrity of the reading and ensures that the process remains respectful and focused. Try to separate your personal feelings from the situation and remain objective.

Communicate Compassionately: Deliver readings with empathy and sensitivity. Tailor your language to be supportive and non-judgmental. Avoid using alarming or overly negative language, and strive to present information in a way that is constructive and empowering.

Be Clear and Honest: Ensure that your readings are clear and honest, but also tactful. If a reading reveals challenging aspects, frame the message in a way that highlights potential solutions or positive aspects. Clarity helps querents understand the message without feeling overwhelmed or misled.

Set Boundaries: Establish clear boundaries regarding the scope of your readings. Let querents know what to expect and avoid overstepping into areas that are beyond your expertise or that may cause unnecessary distress. Try to avoid reading another person who is not present or hasn't given permission to be read.

Dealing with Difficult Readings / Handling Challenging or Negative Readings

1. **Stay Calm and Centered:** When faced with difficult messages, maintain your own emotional composure. Your calm demeanor can help reassure the querent and create a supportive environment for processing the information.
2. **Frame Messages Constructively:** Even if the cards suggest challenging situations, present the information in a way that focuses on potential growth and solutions. For example, instead of merely highlighting problems, offer guidance on how to navigate them and emphasize the strength and resilience of the querent.
3. **Provide Supportive Guidance:** Offer actionable advice and practical steps that the querent can take in response to the reading. This helps transform the reading from a passive experience into an active opportunity for positive change.
4. **Be Compassionate:** Remember that Tarot readings can be emotionally charged. Approach difficult readings with compassion, and be prepared to provide additional support or resources if needed. Sometimes, it may be appropriate to suggest seeking further help from a counselor or therapist, especially if the reading touches on deep emotional issues. It is important to recognize that the reading is providing the information that the querent requires, regardless of your comfort level with providing it.

By adhering to these ethical considerations and best practices, Tarot readers can provide meaningful, respectful, and supportive readings, fostering a positive experience for querents and upholding the integrity of the Tarot practice.

Chapter 8:
Developing Your Tarot Skills

Daily Tarot Practice
The Importance of Daily Practice
Daily Tarot practice is essential for honing your skills and deepening your understanding of the cards. Consistent practice helps you become more familiar with the nuances of the Tarot, enhances your intuition, and strengthens your ability to interpret the cards effectively.

Ideas for Daily Draws
Daily Card Draw: Pull a single card each day to gain insight into the day ahead or to reflect on a specific theme. This practice helps you connect with the energy of the card and observe how its message unfolds throughout your day.

Three-Card Spread: Use a simple three-card spread to explore past, present, and potential outcome of a situation or to gain a broader perspective on your day. This spread provides a more comprehensive view and helps you practice interpreting multiple cards in relation to each other.

Theme-Based Draws: Focus on specific themes such as personal growth, relationships, or career. For example, you might draw a card each day to explore your current emotional state or to seek guidance on a particular goal.

Reflection and Journaling
Tarot Journal: Keep a dedicated Tarot journal to record your daily draws, reflections, and interpretations. Write about the cards you drew, their meanings, and how their messages resonated with your experiences. Over time, your journal

will become a valuable resource for tracking your growth and insights.

Reflections: Spend a few minutes each day reflecting on your card draws. Consider how the messages relate to your daily life and any patterns or recurring themes you notice. Reflecting on your readings helps deepen your understanding and improves your interpretive skills. Be objective and ask your guides to provide you with the answers of the highest purpose / highest good. That includes receiving messages that you don't want to hear. Don't ignore the difficult messages. Often our most powerful growth comes from exploring those shadow sides that we would prefer to discount. What's the point of being psychic if you're not going to pay attention?

Expanding Your Knowledge

Books and Literature

Classic Tarot Books: Explore foundational texts such as "Seventy-Eight Degrees of Wisdom" by Rachel Pollack, "The Tarot Bible" by Sarah Barlett or "Llewellyn's Little Book of Tarot" by Barbara Moore.. These books offer valuable insights into Tarot history, symbolism, and interpretation.

Contemporary Works: Discover modern perspectives and techniques with books like "Modern Tarot" by Michelle Tea, "The Wild Unknown Tarot Guide" by Kim Krans, and "Tarot for Yourself" by Mary K. Greer. These resources provide fresh approaches and innovative practices.

Courses and Workshops

Online Courses: Enroll in online Tarot courses or workshops to learn from experienced readers and instructors. Platforms like Udemy, Coursera, and The Tarot School offer a range of courses covering various aspects of Tarot reading.

Local Workshops: Look for local workshops or meetups where you can connect with other Tarot enthusiasts and gain hands-on experience. These gatherings provide opportunities for practice, feedback, and networking.

Online Communities

Forums and Groups: Join online Tarot forums and communities such as Aeclectic Tarot, Reddit's r/tarot, or Facebook groups dedicated to Tarot. Engaging with these communities allows you to share experiences, seek advice, and learn from others.

Social Media: Follow Tarot readers and educators on platforms like Instagram, YouTube, and TikTok. Many practitioners share valuable content, including tutorials, card interpretations, and spread ideas.

Creating Your Own Tarot Spreads

Designing Personalized Spreads

Identify Your Needs: Start by identifying the specific questions or situations you want to address. Consider what aspects of the situation you want to explore and how many cards you might need to provide a comprehensive view.

Experiment with Layouts: Design custom spreads by arranging cards in patterns that resonate with you. For example, you might create a spread with positions for past influences, current challenges, and future outcomes. Experiment with different layouts and adapt them as needed.

Use Symbols and Themes: Incorporate symbols, themes, or imagery that hold personal significance. For instance, you might design a spread based on the elements (Earth, Air, Fire, Water) or the seasons to reflect different aspects of your life.

Encouragement to Experiment

Trust Your Intuition: Trust your intuition when designing spreads. Allow your creativity to guide you and explore new ways of arranging and interpreting the cards. The more you experiment, the more you'll discover what works best for you.

Reflect and Refine: After using a custom spread, reflect on its effectiveness and make any necessary adjustments. Over time, you'll develop a collection of spreads tailored to your unique style and preferences.

By incorporating daily practice, expanding your knowledge, and creating personalized spreads, you'll continue to grow as a Tarot reader and deepen your connection with the cards. Embrace the journey of learning and exploration, and enjoy the process of discovering new insights and perspectives along the way.

Major Arcana

The Fool
Impulsive, Innocence, Childlike, Pure

The Fool represents new beginnings and a fresh, uninhibited approach to life. With innocence and a childlike wonder, The Fool is ready to take a leap of faith, embracing adventure without fear. This card encourages you to be spontaneous and carefree, trusting in the journey ahead. It symbolizes a pure, untainted perspective, urging you to embrace the unknown with an open heart and a light spirit.

Reversed Meaning

When The Fool appears reversed, it often suggests caution against impulsiveness and reckless behavior. Instead of the carefree adventure the upright card represents, the reversed Fool may indicate naivety, poor judgment, or the potential for taking unnecessary risks. It can also signal hesitation or fear of the unknown, where the querent might be holding back from making a necessary leap due to doubt or insecurity. The reversed Fool warns against being too impulsive or careless, urging you to think things through before acting and to avoid foolish mistakes or missteps.

The Magician
Manifestation, Creation, Confidence

The Magician embodies the power of manifestation and the ability to bring dreams into reality. This card signifies the confidence to focus on a goal and make it happen, utilizing all available resources. The tools (Pentacles, Cups, Swords and Wands) are all on the table before him. It's a card of action, reminding you that you have the ability to turn ideas into reality through focused intent and determination.

Reversed Meaning

When The Magician appears reversed, it often signals a misuse of power, manipulation, or deceit. Instead of manifesting positive outcomes, the reversed Magician may indicate a lack of focus, direction, or confidence, leading to missed opportunities or unfulfilled potential. It can also suggest being out of touch with one's abilities, either overestimating or underestimating them, or using them for selfish purposes. This card warns against trickery, illusion, and the danger of not using your skills and resources wisely.

The High Priestess
Intuition, Unconscious Power, Developing Gifts, Hidden Feelings

The High Priestess represents the deep, mysterious aspects of the unconscious mind and intuition. This card signifies the power of intuition, urging you to trust your instincts and inner wisdom. It is a reminder to look beyond the surface and see what is hidden, as there are deeper truths and insights waiting to be discovered. The High Priestess also suggests the development of spiritual gifts and the importance of connecting with your inner self to uncover hidden feelings and knowledge.

Reversed Meaning

When The High Priestess appears reversed, it indicates a disconnection from intuition and inner wisdom. You may be ignoring your instincts, struggling with self-doubt, or feeling disconnected from your inner voice. This card can also suggest that secrets or hidden information are being withheld, either by yourself or others, leading to confusion or mistrust. The reversed High Priestess warns against relying too much on external validation or neglecting your own inner guidance.

The Empress
Compassion, Nurturing, Fertility

The Empress embodies the energy of nurturing, compassion, and abundance. She is the symbol of fertility, creativity, and the nurturing forces that help ideas, relationships, and projects to grow and flourish. The Empress nurtures the soul, guiding it towards growth and fulfillment, and represents a deep harmony with the natural world. Often seen as the Divine Mother, she brings love, comfort, and a sense of security, encouraging you to embrace your creative potential and to care for yourself and others with warmth and compassion.

Reversed Meaning

When The Empress appears reversed, it suggests a blockage in nurturing energy, either towards yourself or others. This can manifest as neglect, lack of self-care, or feeling disconnected from your creativity and natural instincts. The reversed Empress may indicate issues with fertility, creativity, or abundance, such as creative blocks or smothering relationships.

The Emperor
Power, Authority, Leadership, Security

The Emperor symbolizes structure, stability, and the power of authority. He embodies leadership and the ability to establish order, law, and discipline in life. As a father figure, The Emperor represents assertive thinking, guiding with a firm hand and providing security through clear rules and boundaries. This card encourages you to take control, be decisive, and lead with confidence, whether in personal endeavors or within a larger group. The Emperor's energy is about building a solid foundation, maintaining order, and protecting what has been established.

Reversed Meaning

When The Emperor appears reversed, it indicates a disruption in authority, control, or structure. This can manifest as excessive control, rigidity, or dominance, where power is misused or abused. Alternatively, it may point to a lack of leadership, discipline, or direction, leading to chaos or insecurity. The reversed Emperor suggests that you may be struggling with authority figures or feeling powerless in a situation. It can also indicate challenges with establishing boundaries or maintaining order.

The Hierophant
Respect, Teacher, Ceremony, Conforming, Tradition

The Hierophant represents tradition, conformity, and spiritual guidance. As a teacher and keeper of knowledge, this card embodies respect for established institutions and rituals. It signifies studying higher values, seeking wisdom, and adhering to conventional practices and beliefs. The Hierophant encourages you to align with traditional values, seek guidance from mentors, and participate in ceremonies that reinforce your connection to spiritual and societal structures.

Reversed Meaning

When The Hierophant appears reversed, it often signifies a challenge to traditional values or institutions. It can indicate a departure from conventional beliefs or practices, leading to nonconformity or rebellion against established norms. This card may suggest a need to question or reassess traditional teachings, perhaps due to their limitations or irrelevance to your current situation.

The Lovers
Love, Completeness, Communication, Commitment, Union

The Lovers card embodies the essence of love, commitment, and the profound connection between individuals. It signifies a harmonious union where communication is open and heartfelt. This card often represents the completion and fulfillment found in relationships, whether romantic or otherwise, and emphasizes the importance of making choices that align with your true desires. The Lovers encourages you to embrace love and commitment fully, communicate openly, and seek a deep, meaningful connection that brings a sense of completeness and unity.

Reversed Meaning

When The Lovers appears reversed, it often signals challenges or conflicts in relationships and decision-making. It may indicate misalignment or disharmony in a partnership, issues with communication, or a lack of commitment. The card can suggest difficulties in making choices or a sense of being disconnected from your true desires and values. Reversed, The Lovers may also highlight problems with maintaining a harmonious relationship.

The Chariot
Diligence, Willpower, Perseverance, Determined, Controlled

The Chariot symbolizes triumph through determination and willpower. It represents being in control and confidently steering your life towards your goals, despite challenges. This card reflects a mental and physical journey where persistence and focus are key. The Chariot encourages you to maintain direction and stay committed, even when faced with opposing forces or distractions. It highlights the importance of balancing and directing your energies.

Reversed Meaning

When The Chariot appears reversed, it often signals a loss of control or direction. You may be experiencing difficulties in maintaining focus, discipline, or motivation, leading to feelings of being pulled in multiple directions or struggling to overcome obstacles. The reversed Chariot suggests challenges with asserting willpower and might indicate a need to reassess your goals and strategy.

Strength
Strength, Courage, Self-Awareness

The Strength card embodies inner fortitude, courage, and the power of self-awareness. It signifies taking control and handling challenges with grace and resilience. This card highlights the importance of being responsible for your actions and managing your instincts with patience and compassion. Strength encourages you to harness your inner power, face difficulties bravely, and approach situations with confidence and understanding, demonstrating that true strength comes from within and is rooted in self-awareness and emotional control.

Reversed Meaning

When the Strength card appears reversed, it often points to a lack of inner strength or self-confidence. You may be struggling with fear, insecurity, or feelings of inadequacy, leading to difficulties in managing challenges or controlling your impulses. The reversed Strength card can also indicate a misuse of power or an inability to assert yourself effectively. It may suggest that you are feeling overwhelmed, lacking courage, or failing to take responsibility for your actions.

The Hermit
Discernment, Reflection, Meditation, Withdrawal

The Hermit represents a journey inward, emphasizing discernment and introspection. This card signifies a period of reflection and meditation, where one seeks inner wisdom and guidance. The Hermit encourages withdrawing from external distractions to find direction and clarity within oneself. It may also indicate a fear of revealing a secret or a need for solitude to gain deeper understanding. This card highlights the value of inner exploration and the wisdom gained through personal contemplation and quietude.

Reversed Meaning

When The Hermit appears reversed, it often suggests isolation or withdrawal to the point of disconnection. You may be avoiding self-reflection, resisting inner guidance, or feeling lost without direction. The reversed Hermit can indicate difficulties in finding clarity or wisdom, or an unwillingness to confront personal truths. It might also point to an overemphasis on solitude, leading to loneliness or social disconnection.

The Wheel of Fortune
Luck, Inevitability, Destiny, Turning Point

The Wheel of Fortune represents the cycles of life and the constant change inherent in our experiences. It signifies luck and destiny, highlighting moments of significant turning points and the inevitability of change. This card emphasizes that the only constant is change and encourages you to go with the flow, embracing the patterns and synchronicities that come your way. It often indicates that events are unfolding in alignment with a larger plan, and suggests being open to the shifts and opportunities that arise as part of the natural cycles of life.

Reversed Meaning

When The Wheel of Fortune appears reversed, it often indicates resistance to change or feeling stuck in a cycle of misfortune. You may be experiencing setbacks, delays, or a sense of being out of control, struggling against the natural flow of events. The reversed Wheel of Fortune can suggest difficulties in adapting to changes or patterns repeating in a negative way. It encourages you to reevaluate your approach, remain flexible, and seek to break free from stagnation. It often indicates that events are unfolding in alignment with a larger plan, and suggests being open to the shifts and opportunities that arise as part of the natural cycles of life.

Justice
Fairness, Harmony, Equality

The Justice card represents the principles of fairness, balance, and equality. It emphasizes the importance of objective thinking and making decisions based on truth and integrity. This card highlights the need to communicate openly, listen to all perspectives, and weigh different sides of a situation to restore harmony and achieve just outcomes. The Justice card also signifies taking responsibility for your choices and actions, ensuring that decisions are made with a sense of duty and respect for fairness.

Reversed Meaning

When The Justice card appears reversed, it often indicates issues with fairness, accountability, or integrity. You may be facing imbalances, injustices, or a lack of transparency in a situation. This card can signal dishonesty, bias, or unresolved conflicts where decisions are not being made objectively.

The Hanged Man
Limbo, Transition, Paradox, Perspective

The Hanged Man represents a period of limbo or transition where you may feel stuck or suspended. This card emphasizes the need to see things from a different angle, gaining new perspectives by relinquishing control and accepting a pause or delay. It suggests that you may be bored or dissatisfied with your current situation, but that this time of stagnation can offer valuable insights and opportunities for growth. The Hanged Man encourages embracing this period of suspension to reflect, reevaluate, and shift your perspective to better understand and navigate your circumstances.

Reversed Meaning

When The Hanged Man appears reversed, it often signifies a reluctance to embrace change or an inability to see things from a new perspective. You may be struggling with resistance to letting go or feeling stuck in a rut, unable to move forward or accept necessary transitions. The reversed Hanged Man can indicate frustration with the current situation or a sense of being trapped by your own choices.

The Death Card
Transformation, Change, New Beginnings, Endings

The Death card symbolizes profound transformation and the end of a significant phase or chapter in your life. It represents the process of letting go of the old to make way for new beginnings and growth. This card emphasizes accepting inevitable change, parting ways with the past, and embracing the opportunities that arise from transformation. The Death card encourages you to release what no longer serves you, make peace with endings, and look forward to the fresh starts and possibilities that follow.

Reversed Meaning

When The Death card appears reversed, it often indicates resistance to change or difficulty letting go of the past. You may be clinging to old patterns, relationships, or situations that are no longer serving you, which can hinder your growth and transformation. The reversed Death card suggests that you might be struggling with accepting inevitable changes or facing delays in moving forward. It encourages you to confront and release these resistances.

The Temperance Card
Self-Control, Moderation, Virtue, Compromise
The Temperance card represents balance, moderation, and the art of blending different elements to achieve harmony. It signifies the importance of self-control and finding a middle ground in various aspects of life. This card emphasizes the value of cooperation, compromise, and understanding to create a harmonious and balanced approach. Temperance encourages you to practice moderation and recognize the benefits of integrating diverse perspectives and qualities to foster a sense of inner peace and external harmony.

Reversed Meaning
When The Temperance card appears reversed, it often indicates a lack of balance or difficulties in moderation. You may be struggling with excess, impulsiveness, or conflicts that disrupt harmony and compromise. The reversed Temperance card suggests challenges in integrating different aspects of your life or relationships, leading to disharmony and frustration.

The Devil Card
Temptation, Ignorance of Situation, Materialism, Hedonism
The Devil card represents temptation, materialism, and the darker aspects of human nature. It signifies being trapped in obsessive or addictive patterns of behavior and negative thinking. This card often highlights self-imposed bondage or a lack of freedom due to unhealthy attachments or deceptive situations. The Devil encourages you to confront and break free from these limitations, recognizing where you may be deceiving yourself or indulging in excess. It also reminds you to balance fun and enjoyment with mindful awareness, avoiding the pitfalls of hedonism and materialism.

Reversed Meaning
When The Devil card appears reversed, it signifies liberation from the constraints of unhealthy patterns or addictions. It often indicates a period of overcoming temptation, breaking free from materialism, or addressing negative thinking. The reversed Devil suggests that you are starting to recognize and release self-imposed bondage or deception, leading to greater personal freedom and empowerment.

The Tower Card
External Disruption, Unexpected Events, Revelation
The Tower card represents sudden and dramatic upheaval, often resulting in a major shift in circumstances. It signifies unexpected events or revelations that can disrupt the status quo and force a breakdown of old structures or beliefs. While this card may indicate challenging or chaotic changes, it also heralds the opportunity for new beginnings and growth. The Tower encourages you to embrace the transformative power of these disruptions, understanding that they can clear the way for significant personal or external changes, leading to renewal and progress. Look for opportunities to rebuild the foundation.

Reversed Meaning
When The Tower card appears reversed, it often signifies resistance to change or a reluctance to confront necessary disruptions. You may be avoiding or delaying the inevitable upheaval, leading to a build-up of tension or the potential for an eventual, more chaotic breakdown. The reversed Tower can indicate a fear of change or an attempt to cling to outdated structures, even though they are no longer serving you. It encourages you to address underlying issues and accept that facing and embracing change is crucial for growth and renewal.

The Star Card
Inspiration, Hope, Self-Love, Truth Revealed
The Star card embodies a sense of hope, inspiration, and renewal. It signifies a period of clarity and optimism, where new insights into self-worth and personal value emerge. This card represents confidence in your abilities and a realization of your ideals, offering a light at the end of the tunnel during challenging times. The Star encourages you to embrace self-love, trust in your path, and remain hopeful for a brighter future. It's a reminder that truth is revealed and that a sense of peace and inspiration can guide you forward.

Reversed Meaning
When The Star card appears reversed, it often indicates a period of disillusionment or a loss of hope. You may be experiencing a lack of inspiration, feeling disconnected from your ideals, or struggling with self-doubt. The reversed Star suggests difficulties in seeing the light at the end of the tunnel or challenges in maintaining confidence and optimism.

The Moon Card
Intuition, Goddess Energy, Illusion

The Moon card represents the realm of intuition, mystery, and the unconscious mind. It highlights the importance of trusting your inner guidance and embracing the deeper, often hidden aspects of your psyche. This card signifies exploring the darker side of the soul and recognizing that illusions and uncertainties are a natural part of life. The Moon encourages you to navigate through the fog of confusion with faith in your intuitive insights and to embrace the mystical and enigmatic elements that influence your journey.

Reversed Meaning

When The Moon card appears reversed, it often signifies confusion, illusions, or a lack of clarity. You may be experiencing heightened fears or anxieties that obscure your perception, making it difficult to trust your intuition or see things clearly. The reversed Moon suggests that hidden truths or deceptive situations may be coming to light, prompting you to confront and address underlying issues. It encourages you to overcome misunderstandings and seek clarity, focusing on resolving inner conflicts and gaining a more grounded perspective.

The Sun Card
Joy, Positive Growth, Happiness, Masculine Energy, Communication

The Sun card represents a time of joy, positivity, and significant growth. It signifies happiness, self-confidence, and the celebration of achievements. This card embodies the vibrant energy of masculine power and clear communication, highlighting moments when you are in the spotlight and thriving. The Sun encourages you to embrace your accomplishments with pride, enjoy the abundance of positive experiences, and radiate confidence and optimism. It's a reminder that good times and success are at hand, and that you are shining brightly in all aspects of your life.

Reversed Meaning

When The Sun card appears reversed, it often indicates a period of temporary setbacks or a lack of clarity and joy. You may be experiencing feelings of disappointment or struggling to find optimism and positivity. The reversed Sun suggests challenges in achieving your goals, or difficulties in recognizing and celebrating your accomplishments. It may also signify issues with self-confidence or a sense of being overshadowed.

The Judgement Card
Inner Calling, Awakening, Liberation, Accountability
The Judgement card represents a profound moment of awakening and self-discovery. It signifies a period of inner calling and liberation, where you experience significant realizations or insights. This card often highlights the process of letting go of outdated values and embracing new perspectives. It emphasizes accountability and the need to reflect on and take responsibility for past actions. The Judgement card encourages you to embrace personal growth, make important decisions with clarity, and move forward with a renewed sense of purpose and understanding.

Reversed Meaning
When The Judgement card appears reversed, it often signifies a period of resistance to change or difficulty in facing personal truths. You may be avoiding self-reflection, struggling with self-doubt, or feeling a lack of clarity about your direction. The reversed Judgement card can indicate an unwillingness to release old values or past grievances, leading to stagnation or an inability to move forward. It encourages you to confront and resolve any unresolved issues, take responsibility for past actions, and embrace the need for personal growth and transformation to achieve a sense of renewal and clarity.

The World Card
Completion, Fulfillment, Accomplishment
The World card signifies the achievement of completion and fulfillment. It represents a sense of accomplishment and the successful realization of your goals. This card highlights moments of celebration and feeling at one with yourself and the universe. It suggests that you have reached a significant milestone and that you have the whole world at your fingertips. The World encourages you to embrace your success, enjoy the rewards of your efforts, and recognize the interconnectedness of all aspects of your life.

Reversed Meaning
When The World card appears reversed, it often signifies incomplete projects, unfulfilled goals, or a sense of being stuck in a cycle. You may be experiencing delays, frustrations, or a lack of closure regarding certain aspects of your life. The reversed World can indicate challenges in achieving a sense of completion or feeling disconnected from your sense of purpose.

Minor Arcana

Ace of Pentacles
Gift of Health, Wealth

The Ace of Pentacles represents the potential for new beginnings in the realms of health, wealth, and material success. This card signifies a tangible gift or opportunity, such as an inflow of money, improved well-being, or a chance to establish a stable foundation. It encourages you to stay grounded and seize the opportunity to manifest prosperity and abundance in your life. The Ace of Pentacles is a reminder that with focus and effort, you can turn potential into reality.

Reversed Meaning

When the Ace of Pentacles appears reversed, it often indicates missed opportunities or delays in financial or material gains. You may be experiencing setbacks related to money, health, or a new venture. This card can also suggest a lack of grounding, leading to instability or difficulty manifesting your goals. The reversed Ace of Pentacles encourages you to reassess your plans, be cautious with your resources, and focus on regaining balance to overcome obstacles and achieve the prosperity you seek.

Two of Pentacles
Duality

The Two of Pentacles represents the delicate balance and juggling act required to manage various aspects of life, such as home, career, finances, and health. This card signifies the need to maintain equilibrium while handling multiple responsibilities or making decisions that require careful consideration. It highlights the duality in life, where you're constantly balancing priorities and adapting to changes. The Two of Pentacles encourages flexibility, adaptability, and the ability to manage competing demands effectively.

Reversed Meaning

When the Two of Pentacles appears reversed, it suggests that you may be struggling to maintain balance in your life. You could be feeling overwhelmed by the demands of juggling multiple responsibilities, leading to stress or poor decision-making. This card can indicate financial instability, difficulty managing time, or neglecting important aspects of your life, such as health or relationships. The reversed Two of Pentacles encourages you to reassess your priorities, delegate tasks where possible, and find a more sustainable way to manage your commitments.

Three of Pentacles
Graduation
The Three of Pentacles represents the recognition and reward that comes from hard work and dedication. This card signifies a stage of accomplishment, where your efforts and skills are acknowledged by others. It highlights the importance of teamwork, collaboration, and the successful application of your talents. The Three of Pentacles encourages you to take pride in your achievements and continue refining your craft as you build towards greater success and mastery.
Reversed Meaning
When the Three of Pentacles appears reversed, it often indicates issues with teamwork, lack of recognition, or a failure to meet expectations. You may be experiencing challenges in collaborating with others, or feeling undervalued for your contributions. This card can also suggest a lack of progress, poor workmanship, or difficulties in mastering a particular skill. The reversed Three of Pentacles encourages you to reassess your approach, improve communication, and focus on developing your abilities to achieve the recognition and success you seek.

Four of Pentacles
Protecting Assets
The Four of Pentacles represents a strong focus on financial security and the desire to protect your assets. This card often suggests a tendency to hold onto resources tightly, sometimes to the point of being miserly or overly cautious. It highlights the importance of being in control of your material wealth and safeguarding what you have worked hard to achieve. The Four of Pentacles encourages you to find a balance between maintaining security and being open to new opportunities or experiences.
Reversed Meaning
When the Four of Pentacles appears reversed, it suggests a loosening of your grip on material possessions or financial security. You may be experiencing a release of control, letting go of rigid attitudes towards money, or overcoming fears related to scarcity. This card can also indicate financial instability, reckless spending, or a lack of concern for security. The reversed card encourages you to find a healthier balance between holding on and letting go, and to reassess your relationship with wealth and security to ensure it serves your long-term well-being.

Five of Pentacles
Suffering
The Five of Pentacles represents hardship, struggle, and a sense of loss or lack. This card often signifies feelings of isolation, financial difficulty, or emotional distress. It highlights the suffering that comes from focusing on what is missing rather than what is available. The key message of the Five of Pentacles is to look up and see the light, recognizing that even in times of adversity, support and resources are within your grasp. It encourages you to shift from a victim mentality to one of resilience and to seek help or new perspectives to overcome challenges.

Reversed Meaning
When the Five of Pentacles appears reversed, it suggests a recovery from hardship or a gradual improvement in your situation. You may be finding your way out of financial difficulties, emotional struggles, or a period of isolation. This card indicates a renewed sense of hope and the possibility of regaining stability. The reversed Five of Pentacles encourages you to recognize the support around you and to embrace opportunities for growth and healing.

Six of Pentacles
Generosity
The Six of Pentacles represents the themes of generosity, balance, and the sharing of resources. This card highlights acts of kindness, philanthropy, and the giving and receiving of support, whether in terms of health, wealth, or other forms of assistance. It emphasizes the importance of equitable exchange and the need to maintain a balance between giving and receiving. The Six of Pentacles also suggests a focus on fairness and judgement, indicating that your actions and decisions should be guided by a sense of equality and compassion.

Reversed Meaning
When the Six of Pentacles appears reversed, it often signifies issues with imbalance in giving and receiving. You may be experiencing unfairness, exploitation, or a lack of generosity, either from others or in your own actions. This card can indicate that you or someone else is struggling with issues related to charity, financial support, or unequal exchanges.

Seven of Pentacles
Be Patient for Growth
The Seven of Pentacles signifies a period of evaluation and patience. It represents the hard work and effort you've invested in a project or goal and the anticipation of future results. This card highlights the importance of waiting for your efforts to bear fruit and understanding that growth takes time. It encourages you to assess your progress and make any necessary adjustments, recognizing that the rewards will come with persistence and patience. The Seven of Pentacles also prompts reflection on whether your work aligns with your long-term goals and whether you are working to live or living to work.

Reversed Meaning
When the Seven of Pentacles appears reversed, it often indicates frustration or impatience with slow progress and lack of immediate results. You may feel disillusioned or discouraged by the perceived lack of rewards from your hard work. This card can suggest a need to reassess your goals, approach, or efforts, and possibly address any misalignment between your actions and long-term objectives. It encourages you to reflect on whether your investment of time and energy is truly serving your best interests and to be open to making adjustments for more effective outcomes.

Eight of Pentacles
Diligence
The Eight of Pentacles represents dedication, skill development, and hard work. It signifies a period of focused effort where your attention to detail and commitment to mastering your craft or trade are paying off. This card highlights the importance of staying on track and continuing to refine your skills, as your diligence and perseverance will lead to tangible results and accomplishments. It encourages you to keep up the good work, maintain your discipline, and take pride in the progress you're making.

Reversed Meaning
When the Eight of Pentacles appears reversed, it often indicates a lack of focus, discipline, or dedication in your work. You may be experiencing frustration or feeling unmotivated, leading to unfinished projects or a decline in the quality of your efforts. This card can suggest issues with commitment or a need to reassess your goals and methods.

Nine of Pentacles
I've Arrived
The Nine of Pentacles signifies a sense of achievement and personal success. This card represents reaching a level of accomplishment and financial stability by your own standards, often through hard work and self-sufficiency. It highlights the rewards of your efforts, including financial security, independence, and a comfortable lifestyle. The image of the hawk hooded in the card symbolizes control and mastery, indicating that you have harnessed your resources and skills effectively. The Nine of Pentacles encourages you to enjoy the fruits of your labor and take pride in your accomplishments.

Reversed Meaning
When the Nine of Pentacles appears reversed, it often suggests issues with financial security or self-sufficiency. You may be experiencing a sense of instability, dependency, or a lack of fulfillment despite your efforts. This card can indicate challenges in maintaining your standard of living or a feeling of not measuring up to your own expectations. It encourages you to reassess your priorities, address any financial or personal imbalances, and work towards reclaiming your independence and sense of accomplishment.

Ten of Pentacles
All is Well in The Kingdom
The Ten of Pentacles signifies a sense of fulfillment, stability, and abundance. It represents the culmination of efforts and the enjoyment of a bountiful harvest, symbolizing financial success, family harmony, and long-term security. This card highlights the appreciation of what you have built and achieved, reflecting a period of contentment and prosperity. The Ten of Pentacles encourages you to value and celebrate the stability and wealth you have created, as well as to cherish the support and legacy of your family and community.

Reversed Meaning
When the Ten of Pentacles appears reversed, it often indicates issues with financial stability, family dynamics, or long-term security. You may be facing challenges related to inheritance, familial disputes, or a lack of fulfillment despite previous successes. This card can suggest instability or difficulties in maintaining the wealth and legacy you have worked for.

Page of Pentacles
Apprentice
The Page of Pentacles represents new beginnings, learning, and the pursuit of practical goals. This card symbolizes a youthful enthusiasm for acquiring knowledge, developing skills, and laying the groundwork for future success. It highlights a period of study, growth, and exploration in areas related to finance, work, or personal development. The Page of Pentacles encourages you to embrace new opportunities with curiosity and diligence, and to remain focused on your long-term aspirations as you build your foundation for success.

Reversed Meaning
When the Page of Pentacles appears reversed, it often indicates challenges related to focus, discipline, or the practical aspects of your goals. You may be struggling with procrastination, lack of direction, or difficulty in following through with your plans. This card can suggest missed opportunities, lack of commitment, or a need to reevaluate your approach to learning and personal growth. It encourages you to address any obstacles, and work on developing the necessary skills and discipline to move forward effectively.

Knight of Pentacles
Defender
The Knight of Pentacles represents reliability, hard work, and a steadfast approach to achieving goals. This card symbolizes a disciplined and methodical individual who is committed to their responsibilities and diligent in their efforts. As a defender, the Knight of Pentacles stands firm in protecting and maintaining their values, finances, or work. It highlights a strong sense of duty, perseverance, and practical action. The Knight of Pentacles encourages you to stay focused on your tasks, be patient in your endeavors, and approach challenges with a steady and dependable mindset.

Reversed Meaning
When the Knight of Pentacles appears reversed, it often indicates issues with commitment, discipline, or progress. You may be experiencing delays, lack of motivation, or feeling stuck in your responsibilities. This card can suggest a tendency toward rigidity, over-cautiousness, or an inability to adapt to changing circumstances. It encourages you to address any obstacles to progress, re-evaluate your approach, and work on regaining your motivation and flexibility.

Queen of Pentacles
Midwife

The Queen of Pentacles represents nurturing, practicality, and resourcefulness. As a midwife, she symbolizes the ability to support and care for others, creating a stable and nurturing environment for growth and development. This card highlights qualities of compassion, financial acumen, and a deep connection to the home and family. The Queen of Pentacles encourages you to embrace your role as a caretaker and provider, utilizing your resources and skills to foster prosperity and well-being for yourself and those around you.

Reversed Meaning

When the Queen of Pentacles appears reversed, it often indicates issues with nurturing, stability, or self-care. You may be struggling with imbalances in your responsibilities, financial instability, or difficulties in managing your home and personal life. This card can suggest a tendency toward being overly controlling, neglecting self-care, or feeling disconnected from your practical and emotional needs. It encourages you to address any areas of imbalance, reassess your approach to caregiving and medical concerns, and work on restoring harmony and stability in your life.

King of Pentacles
Provider, Protector

The King of Pentacles represents mastery, stability, and financial success. As a provider and protector, he embodies the qualities of leadership, responsibility, and security. This card signifies a strong and dependable individual who excels in managing resources, building wealth, and creating a solid foundation for others. The King of Pentacles highlights the importance of practical wisdom, strategic thinking, and the ability to offer support and protection.

Reversed Meaning

When the King of Pentacles appears reversed, it often indicates issues with stability, responsibility, or financial management. You may be facing challenges related to mismanagement of resources, insecurity, or a lack of practicality. This card can suggest problems with being overly controlling, materialistic, or neglectful in providing for others. It encourages you to address any financial or leadership issues, reassess your approach to wealth and responsibility, and work on restoring balance and integrity in your role as a provider.

Ace of Cups
Gift of Love
The Ace of Cups represents the beginning of emotional growth and the gift of love. It signifies new emotional opportunities, such as the birth of a deep connection, creative inspiration, or a fresh perspective on handling feelings. This card highlights the potential for profound emotional experiences, whether through new relationships, personal insights, or a renewed sense of compassion. The Ace of Cups encourages you to embrace and nurture these new emotional beginnings, allowing them to enrich your life and foster deeper connections with yourself and others.
Reversed Meaning
When the Ace of Cups appears reversed, it often indicates emotional blockages, unfulfilled potential, or difficulties with expressing feelings. You may be experiencing issues related to emotional stagnation, repressed emotions, or a lack of connection with your inner self. This card can suggest challenges in forming new relationships or a need to address unresolved emotional issues. It encourages you to work on opening up emotionally, clearing any blockages, and finding healthy ways to express and process your feelings.

Two of Cups
Relationship
The Two of Cups represents the harmonious coming together of people, ideas, or emotions. It signifies a deep connection, mutual respect, and a balanced partnership. This card highlights the formation of meaningful relationships, whether romantic, platonic, or professional, where both parties share a genuine bond and emotional exchange. The Two of Cups encourages you to embrace and nurture these connections, focusing on cooperation and mutual support.
Reversed Meaning
When the Two of Cups appears reversed, it often indicates challenges or disharmony in relationships. You may be experiencing issues with communication, misalignment of emotions, or a lack of mutual understanding. This card can suggest difficulties in forming or maintaining connections, whether romantic, platonic, or professional. It encourages you to address any conflicts or misunderstandings, work on improving communication, and strive to restore balance and harmony in your relationships.

Three of Cups
Celebrate Friends

The Three of Cups signifies celebration, joy, and the positive impact of friendships. It represents moments of sharing, communal gatherings, and the supportive bonds between friends. This card highlights the importance of coming together with loved ones to celebrate achievements, milestones, or simply the joy of companionship. It encourages you to embrace social connections, express gratitude, and enjoy the happiness that comes from shared experiences and support. The Three of Cups is a reminder to cherish and nurture your relationships with those who bring you joy.

Reversed Meaning

When the Three of Cups appears reversed, it often indicates issues with social connections or celebrations. You may be experiencing feelings of isolation, disconnection, or dissatisfaction with your friendships or social life. This card can suggest misunderstandings, conflicts, or a lack of harmony in group settings. It encourages you to address any issues within your social circles, work on resolving conflicts, and find ways to reconnect with others.

Four of Cups
Acceptance

The Four of Cups represents a period of contemplation and the need for acceptance. It often signifies being in a state of introspection, where you may be feeling disconnected or unfulfilled despite the opportunities or gifts being offered to you. This card suggests that you are focused on past disappointments or current dissatisfaction, which may be causing you to overlook new possibilities. The Four of Cups encourages you to open yourself up to new opportunities and to embrace the gifts being offered, while also reflecting on your current state and finding a way to move forward with acceptance and gratitude.

Reversed Meaning

When the Four of Cups appears reversed, it often indicates a shift in perspective or an awakening to new opportunities. You may be emerging from a period of stagnation or introspection, becoming more open and receptive to the possibilities around you. This card suggests a readiness to embrace change, explore new options, and overcome previous dissatisfaction or disconnection.

Five of Cups
Grief
The Five of Cups represents a period of mourning and emotional distress. It signifies dealing with loss, regret, or disappointment, and the process of coming to terms with these feelings. This card highlights the importance of allowing yourself time to grieve and acknowledging your emotions. It encourages you to process your feelings fully, understanding that healing takes time. While focusing on what has been lost or missed, the Five of Cups also reminds you to recognize and appreciate the remaining positive aspects of your life.

Reversed Meaning
When the Five of Cups appears reversed, it often signifies the process of moving past grief and finding healing. You may be beginning to let go of past disappointments and shifting your focus toward recovery and rebuilding. This card indicates a potential for emotional renewal and the ability to see the positives in your situation, even if it's been difficult. It suggests that you are starting to embrace hope, forgiveness, and new perspectives, allowing yourself to move forward and find closure.

Six of Cups
Inner Child
The Six of Cups represents nostalgia, childhood memories, and the inner child. It signifies a connection to your past, recalling fond memories, and the joy of simpler times. This card highlights the importance of revisiting and healing old emotional wounds or reconnecting with your youthful enthusiasm and innocence. It encourages you to share your feelings and emotions openly, both with yourself and others, and to communicate clearly about your needs and desires. The Six of Cups reminds you to embrace and nurture your inner child, finding joy and healing through reflection on past experiences and the positive aspects of your personal history.

Reversed Meaning
When the Six of Cups appears reversed, it often indicates difficulties with letting go of the past or issues related to nostalgia and childhood. You may be struggling with unresolved issues from your past or feeling disconnected from your inner child. This card suggests a need to address any lingering emotional baggage or to release old patterns that are no longer serving you.

Seven of Cups
Illusion

The Seven of Cups represents a state of confusion, illusion, and a multitude of choices or fantasies. It signifies the potential for being overwhelmed by options or deceived by unrealistic dreams. This card highlights the need to discern between fantasy and reality and to avoid being misled by illusions. While it suggests that manifestation and creative visualization are possible, it also warns against getting lost in wishful thinking or making decisions based on false hopes.

Reversed Meaning

When the Seven of Cups appears reversed, it often indicates a move towards clarity and decision-making. You may be emerging from a state of confusion or illusion, gaining a clearer understanding of your options and desires. This card suggests a realization of what is truly important and a rejection of unrealistic fantasies.

Eight of Cups
Letting Go

The Eight of Cups represents the act of leaving behind situations, relationships, or conditions that no longer serve you. It signifies a journey of emotional departure and the decision to move on from what is unfulfilling or stagnant. This card highlights the importance of letting go of the past and transforming any grief or dissatisfaction into opportunities for personal growth and renewal. It encourages you to pursue deeper meaning and fulfillment, even if it means making difficult choices or facing the unknown. The Eight of Cups is a reminder to trust in your decision to seek something better and to embrace the process of moving forward.

Reversed Meaning

When the Eight of Cups appears reversed, it often signifies difficulty in letting go or moving on from past situations or relationships. You might be clinging to what no longer serves you, struggling with feelings of hesitation or fear about change. This card suggests a need to address unresolved issues or to confront the reasons why you may be holding onto something that isn't fulfilling. The reversed Eight of Cups encourages you to examine your reluctance to move forward, face your fears, and make the necessary changes to achieve emotional growth and fulfillment. It is a call to overcome obstacles and commit to personal transformation.

Nine of Cups
Surrounded by Love
The Nine of Cups represents a state of emotional fulfillment, satisfaction, and contentment. It signifies having achieved a level of personal happiness and enjoying the love and support from those around you. This card highlights a sense of accomplishment and self-satisfaction, often associated with feeling surrounded by affection and appreciation. It encourages you to recognize and be grateful for the love and blessings you have in your life. However, it also suggests a need to balance this contentment with humility, as excessive pride or smugness may overshadow your genuine happiness.

Reversed Meaning
When the Nine of Cups appears reversed, it often signifies dissatisfaction or a sense of unfulfillment despite outward appearances of success. You may be feeling that your emotional needs are not being fully met, or that there is a gap between your desires and your reality. This card can also indicate overindulgence, vanity, or an excessive focus on material or superficial pleasures, which may lead to a lack of genuine satisfaction.

Ten of Cups
Satisfaction, Emotional Contentment
The Ten of Cups represents a state of profound emotional fulfillment and happiness. It signifies achieving a deep sense of satisfaction and well-being in your personal and familial relationships. This card highlights the joy of harmony and unity with loved ones, reflecting a sense of true happiness and contentment. It symbolizes a harmonious family life or a fulfilling emotional state where all aspects of your relationships and personal life align beautifully. The

Reversed Meaning
When the Ten of Cups appears reversed, it often indicates issues with emotional fulfillment or dissatisfaction in personal relationships. There may be conflicts, misunderstandings, or a sense of disconnection within your family or close relationships. This card can reflect difficulties in achieving the ideal vision of happiness and harmony, or feeling that your emotional needs are not being fully met. It may also point to unrealistic expectations or unresolved issues that are affecting your sense of contentment.

Page of Cups
Creative, Sensitive, Open-hearted

The Page of Cups represents a youthful, imaginative, and emotionally open energy. This card signifies a person who is in touch with their emotions, often exploring creative or intuitive pursuits. It symbolizes new beginnings in matters of the heart or creative ventures, and can indicate a message or opportunity related to emotional or artistic expression.

If interpreted as a "narcissist," it would suggest a focus on self-centered behavior and the need for validation, but this is not a traditional interpretation of the Page of Cups.

Reversed Meaning

When the Page of Cups appears reversed, it often indicates challenges with emotional expression or creative pursuits. You might be experiencing emotional instability, difficulty connecting with your feelings, or a lack of authenticity in your interactions. This card can suggest issues with being overly self-absorbed, insincere, or struggling with a lack of emotional maturity.

Knight of Cups
Romantic, Idealistic, Charming

The Knight of Cups represents a figure who is deeply in touch with their emotions and driven by romantic ideals. This card signifies someone who is passionate, charming, and often seeks to express their feelings through gestures of love and creativity. The Knight of Cups is associated with pursuing dreams and aspirations, especially those related to matters of the heart or artistic endeavors.

If interpreted as a "Casanova," it suggests a charismatic and romantic individual who may be known for their seductive or idealistic approach to relationships. However, it's important to note that this interpretation emphasizes the Knight's romantic and emotional nature rather than purely superficial or manipulative behavior.

Reversed Meaning

When the Knight of Cups appears reversed, it often indicates issues related to emotional instability or unrealistic romantic expectations. This card can suggest being out of touch with one's feelings, engaging in manipulative or deceitful behavior in relationships, or experiencing a lack of direction in pursuing one's emotional or creative goals.

Queen of Cups
Compassionate, Nurturing, Intuitive
The Queen of Cups embodies deep emotional intelligence, empathy, and nurturing qualities. She represents someone who is deeply in touch with their own emotions and those of others, offering support and understanding in a heartfelt manner.

If interpreted as a "soul mate," the Queen of Cups suggests a profound, nurturing connection with another person who provides emotional depth and support. This relationship is characterized by mutual understanding, compassion, and a strong emotional bond.

Reversed Meaning
When the Queen of Cups appears reversed, it often indicates challenges with emotional balance or self-care. This card may reflect issues such as emotional instability, difficulty in managing feelings, or a tendency to become overly dependent on others for emotional support. It can also suggest being out of touch with one's intuitive insights or experiencing a lack of empathy and understanding in relationships.

King of Cups
Emotional Maturity, Compassionate, Balanced
The King of Cups represents emotional maturity and a deep understanding of both one's own feelings and those of others. He embodies qualities of compassion, empathy, and balance, offering support and guidance with a calm and collected demeanor.

If interpreted as "unconditional love," the King of Cups reflects a relationship characterized by profound emotional support and acceptance. This figure represents someone who loves deeply and consistently, regardless of circumstances, and is able to offer a steady and nurturing presence.

Reversed Meaning
When the King of Cups appears reversed, it often indicates difficulties with emotional regulation and maturity. This card may reflect issues such as emotional imbalance, moodiness, or a tendency to avoid dealing with feelings in a constructive way. It can also suggest manipulative or controlling behavior in relationships, where emotional support is not genuine or is used for personal gain.

In a reversed position, the King of Cups encourages you to address these emotional challenges by seeking to understand and manage your feelings more effectively.

Ace of Swords
Clarity, Insight, Truth
The Ace of Swords represents a breakthrough in understanding or clarity. It signifies the arrival of a new idea, insight, or truth that cuts through confusion and brings a clear perspective. This card indicates a powerful mental shift, often involving the discovery of a solution to a problem or an "aha" moment that reveals new possibilities. It embodies the gift of logic, sharp thinking, and the ability to see things clearly, leading to decisive action and intellectual clarity.

Reversed Meaning
When the Ace of Swords appears reversed, it often indicates confusion, miscommunication, or a lack of clarity. This card may suggest that you are struggling to see the truth or find a clear solution to a problem. There may be misunderstandings, mental blockages, or difficulty expressing your thoughts and ideas effectively. It can also reflect delays in gaining insight or encountering obstacles in achieving mental clarity.
In this position, the Ace of Swords encourages you to address these challenges by seeking greater understanding and improving communication.

Two of Swords
Stalemate, Indecision, Inner Conflict
The Two of Swords represents a state of indecision or being stuck between conflicting choices or viewpoints. It often signifies a mental or emotional stalemate where a decision is difficult to make, and you might be feeling blocked or unable to see a clear path forward. This card reflects an inner conflict or a need to reconcile opposing forces within yourself, whether they be thoughts, feelings, or external situations. The Two of Swords encourages you to seek clarity and address any underlying issues that are preventing you from moving forward.

Reversed Meaning
When the Two of Swords appears reversed, it often indicates a shift from a state of indecision or stagnation towards resolution and clarity. This card suggests that you are starting to move past previous blocks or conflicts, leading to a clearer understanding of your choices or situation. It may also signify the release of mental or emotional barriers that were holding you back, allowing for a new perspective or solution to emerge.

Three of Swords
Heartache, Grief, Emotional Pain
The Three of Swords represents emotional pain and heartache, often associated with grief, sorrow, or betrayal. It signifies a period of emotional struggle or distress, where the heart is affected by sadness or loss. This card can highlight the perception of being a victim of circumstances or relationships, and the need to address and process these emotions.
The Three of Swords encourages you to recognize and confront your pain, but also to seek healing and move forward. It prompts you to question whether the pain is more mental or emotional, and to find ways to cope and eventually let go of the suffering to make space for healing and growth.
Reversed Meaning
When the Three of Swords appears reversed, it often indicates a period of healing and recovery following emotional pain or heartbreak. This card suggests that you are starting to process beyond previous sorrow or grief, finding ways to mend your heart and reconcile with past hurts. It may also signify forgiveness, both towards others and yourself, and a gradual release of the lingering emotional wounds.

Four of Swords
Meditation, Rest, Recuperation
The Four of Swords represents a time of rest, meditation, and recuperation. It indicates the need to step back from stress or conflict and take a period of reflection or relaxation to restore your mental and emotional well-being. This card suggests that taking a break or finding a quiet space to meditate and recharge is essential for regaining balance and clarity. The Four of Swords encourages you to pause, reflect, and give yourself the time you need to recover from challenges or exhaustion. It's a call to prioritize self-care and inner peace, allowing yourself to rejuvenate and prepare for the next steps with renewed energy and perspective.
Reversed Meaning
When the Four of Swords appears reversed, it often indicates a period of restlessness or burnout. This card suggests that you may be struggling to take a break or find the peace and relaxation you need. It can point to an inability to slow down, a tendency to overwork, or difficulty in stepping back from stressors to recharge.

Five of Swords
Conflict, Change Ideas, Disruption

The Five of Swords represents conflict, tension, and the potential for misunderstandings or disputes. It often signifies a situation where ideas, achievements, or recognition may be contested or where there is a sense of taking credit for someone else's work. This card can highlight issues of respect and integrity, suggesting that the way you handle conflicts or disagreements may impact relationships.

The Five of Swords encourages you to reflect on how you navigate conflicts and whether you're respecting others' contributions and ideas. It's a call to address any issues of dishonesty or personal responsibility and to strive for resolution with respect and fairness.

Reversed Meaning

When the Five of Swords appears reversed, it often signals a shift towards resolution and reconciliation after a period of conflict or tension. This card indicates that the disputes or disagreements you've experienced may be moving towards a resolution or that you're beginning to seek peace and rebuild relationships. It can also suggest letting go of past grievances and moving on from arguments or misunderstandings.

The reversed Five of Swords encourages you to focus on resolving conflicts constructively and making amends where necessary.

Six of Swords
Transition, Relief, Assistance

The Six of Swords represents a transition or journey from a challenging situation towards a more peaceful state. It symbolizes moving away from difficulties or turmoil and finding relief or support during times of hardship. This card suggests that assistance is available, whether through accepting help from others or providing support to someone in need.

The Six of Swords signifies that challenging times are coming to an end and that progress is being made towards a more stable and serene phase.

Reversed Meaning

When the Six of Swords appears reversed, it often indicates difficulty in moving on from past troubles or a delay in transitioning to a more peaceful state. This card suggests that you might be experiencing resistance to change or struggling to accept help, resulting in lingering problems or an inability to leave behind challenging situations.

Seven of Swords
Deception, Theft, Betrayal

The Seven of Swords represents themes of deception, dishonesty, or betrayal. It often suggests that there may be an element of theft or the feeling that your ideas or solutions are being taken without proper credit. This card can indicate situations where there is a lack of transparency or where someone is acting in a covert or underhanded manner.

The Seven of Swords encourages vigilance and discernment. It's a sign to be cautious about who you trust and to ensure that your contributions and ideas are acknowledged.

Reversed Meaning

When the Seven of Swords appears reversed, it often signifies a move towards honesty and transparency after a period of deceit or hidden agendas. This card suggests that issues of dishonesty or theft are being addressed and resolved. It may indicate that someone is coming clean about their actions, or that you are confronting and resolving issues related to deception. In this position, the Seven of Swords encourages you to face the truth and work on rebuilding trust and integrity.

Eight of Swords
Constraint, Restriction, Powerlessness

The Eight of Swords represents a sense of feeling trapped or restricted, often due to self-imposed limitations or a lack of clarity. It indicates a situation where you may feel bound by your circumstances, unable to see a way out, or paralyzed by fear and uncertainty. The card highlights the feeling of being powerless or stuck, often due to mental or emotional barriers.

This card suggests that while the situation may seem dire, it is often more about perception than reality. The Eight of Swords encourages you to recognize that these constraints might be self-imposed or based on misconceptions.

Reversed Meaning

When the Eight of Swords appears reversed, it signifies a release from feelings of restriction or entrapment. This card suggests that you are beginning to see beyond the limitations or fears that have previously held you back. You are gaining clarity and finding ways to overcome obstacles that once seemed insurmountable.

Nine of Swords
Anxiety, Stress, Nightmares

The Nine of Swords is often associated with intense anxiety, stress, and worry. It depicts a state of mental anguish where you might be losing sleep over a troubling situation or experiencing nightmares. This card highlights the overwhelming nature of your fears and concerns, often amplifying them in your mind.

It suggests that you may be facing significant inner turmoil, and the weight of these worries can feel unbearable. The Nine of Swords encourages you to address these fears directly and seek support or solutions.

Reversed Meaning

When the Nine of Swords appears reversed, it signifies a shift away from intense anxiety and stress. This card suggests that you are beginning to find relief from your worries and are moving towards healing and resolution. You might be starting to address and confront the fears and concerns that have been troubling you, leading to a reduction in their impact on your well-being.

The reversed Nine of Swords indicates that you are making progress in overcoming your anxieties, and it's a sign that you may be able to let go of the negative thought patterns that have been keeping you up at night.

Ten of Swords
Overthinking, Betrayal, Finality

The Ten of Swords often represents a period of intense mental anguish or crisis, where overthinking has reached its peak. This card can indicate a sense of betrayal, failure, or an overwhelming end to a situation. The imagery usually depicts a person lying face-down with ten swords in their back, symbolizing the depth of their struggle.

The Ten of Swords highlights the feeling of being trapped in negative thought patterns or dwelling excessively on past hurts and disappointments. It suggests that while the situation may feel dire, it also marks the end of a challenging phase.

Reversed Meaning

When the Ten of Swords appears reversed, it indicates a period of recovery and the beginning of a new chapter after a difficult or painful experience. This card suggests that while you may have experienced significant challenges or crises, you are now moving away from that period of suffering and starting to rebuild.

Page of Swords
Curiosity, Learning, Communication

The Page of Swords represents a youthful and energetic approach to acquiring knowledge and understanding. This card signifies a period of intellectual curiosity, where you are eager to explore new ideas and gather information. It embodies the spirit of a student or someone who is actively learning and growing.

This card often points to a time of sharp observation and keen insight, where you are ready to communicate your ideas and thoughts with enthusiasm. The Page of Swords encourages you to embrace your curiosity, stay open-minded, and be willing to question and investigate in order to gain deeper understanding.

Reversed Meaning

When the Page of Swords appears reversed, it suggests challenges related to communication, learning, or intellectual pursuits. This card can indicate impulsiveness or a tendency to speak without thinking, which may lead to misunderstandings or conflicts. It might also point to a lack of focus or clarity in your thoughts and communications.

Knight of Swords
Boldness, Action, Intellect

The Knight of Swords represents a dynamic and assertive approach to tackling challenges and pursuing goals. This card signifies someone who is driven by intellect and ideals, often charging forward with determination and clarity of purpose. The Knight of Swords embodies the energy of a warrior armed with ideas, ready to take decisive action to achieve their objectives.

This card highlights the importance of courage and mental agility in overcoming obstacles. It encourages you to harness your intellect and enthusiasm to address issues head-on, while also being mindful of the potential for rashness or impulsiveness. The Knight of Swords is a reminder to balance your bold actions with thoughtful consideration and strategic planning.

Reversed Meaning

When the Knight of Swords appears reversed, it often signals challenges related to impulsiveness and recklessness. This card can indicate a tendency to act without fully considering the consequences, leading to misunderstandings or conflicts. It may also reflect difficulties in communication or a lack of clear direction in your pursuits.

Queen of Swords
Clarity, Independence, Insight
The Queen of Swords represents a figure of clarity and independence. She is known for her sharp intellect, keen insight, and ability to communicate with honesty and precision. This card signifies a person who is not afraid to speak the truth, no matter how uncomfortable it may be, and who values clear and direct communication.
The Queen of Swords embodies the qualities of a discerning and objective thinker. She can cut through confusion and emotional fog to get to the heart of the matter, making decisions based on logic and rationality. effectively.

Reversed Meaning
When the Queen of Swords appears reversed, it can indicate issues related to communication and emotional expression. This card may suggest that you are being overly harsh or critical, or that you are struggling with clarity in your thoughts and communications. There may be a tendency to use sharp words or be emotionally detached, which can create misunderstandings or conflicts. The reversed Queen of Swords warns against letting bitterness or emotional wounds affect your interactions. It may indicate you are being overly critical of yourself or others.

King of Swords
Authority, Intellect, Strategy
The King of Swords embodies authority and intellectual mastery. He is a figure of strategic thinking, clear communication, and ethical leadership. This card represents someone who is adept at using their intellect and analytical skills to navigate complex situations and make informed decisions.
The King of Swords is often seen as a powerful advisor or leader who operates with a high level of integrity and wisdom. He values fairness and justice and uses his intellectual prowess to guide others and solve problems.

Reversed Meaning
When the King of Swords appears reversed, it can indicate issues related to authority and leadership. This card may suggest that someone in a position of power is abusing their authority or acting in a manipulative or dishonest manner. It can also point to a lack of clarity and ethical considerations in decision-making.
The reversed King of Swords warns against the misuse of power and the potential for conflicts arising from unethical behavior or poor judgment.

Ace of Wands
Brilliant Intuition, Gift of Insight
The Ace of Wands represents a powerful surge of energy, creativity, and inspiration. It signals the beginning of a new venture or a burst of enthusiasm that encourages you to take action. This card symbolizes a spark of intuition or insight that feels like a divine gift, urging you to pursue your passions and embrace new opportunities with confidence.

Reversed Meaning
When reversed, the Ace of Wands indicates a blockage in your creative flow or a lack of motivation. You may feel uninspired or unsure of which direction to take, leading to missed opportunities or delays. This card suggests the need to overcome fear, doubt, or confusion to reignite your inner fire and move forward with renewed energy.

Two of Wands
Gateway, Planning, Decisions, Potential
The Two of Wands represents a moment of decision, often involving choices about which direction to take. This card suggests standing at a gateway, contemplating the possibilities ahead. It's a time of planning and envisioning what lies beyond your current situation. Whether it's choosing to stay in a familiar place or venturing into the unknown, the Two of Wands encourages careful consideration of your options and a clear vision of your desired outcome. This card signals the potential for growth and expansion, but only if you make the right choices.

Reversed Meaning
When the Two of Wands is reversed, it indicates a struggle with making decisions and a reluctance to step out of your comfort zone. You may feel uncertain about the future, leading to hesitation and missed opportunities. This card suggests being stuck in a state of indecision, unable to commit to a path or take action. It's a reminder that while planning is important, overthinking can lead to paralysis, and sometimes, taking a risk is necessary to move forward.

Three of Wards
Trust the decision

The Three of Wands Tarot card is a powerful symbol of forward momentum and strategic vision. It represents the moment when you've made a significant decision or embarked on a new journey, and now it's time to trust that choice fully. You've gone through the gateway, leaving behind the familiar and stepping into a world of new opportunities and possibilities. This card encourages you to embrace the path ahead with confidence and determination, knowing that your efforts and planning have set the stage for success. The Three of Wands reminds you not to look back or second-guess your decisions.

Reversed Meaning

The reversed Three of Wands Tarot card indicates delays, obstacles, or a lack of foresight in your plans. It suggests that you may be struggling to see the bigger picture, leading to frustration and setbacks. You might feel stuck or unsure about the direction you're heading in, possibly due to a lack of planning or unrealistic expectations. This card warns against impulsive decisions and advises you to reassess your approach before moving forward.

Four of Wands
Celebrate Insight

The Four of Wands Tarot card is a symbol of celebration, stability, and the joy that comes from achieving a significant milestone. It represents a time of harmony and unity, where you can pause to appreciate the progress you've made and the solid foundation you've built. The Four of Wands also carries the energy of insight and understanding. It is a reminder to trust your instincts and the wisdom that comes from deep within. The card suggests that you have been given a gift of clarity, allowing you to see the bigger picture and understand the deeper meaning of your experiences. Don't doubt your instincts; they are guiding you toward what feels right and true.

Reversed Meaning

The reversed Four of Wands Tarot card suggests instability or a lack of harmony, often in situations where celebration and unity would normally be expected. There may be disruptions in your plans, such as canceled events, delayed milestones, or conflicts within a group or community.

Five of Wands
Battle for beliefs
The Five of Wands Tarot card represents conflict, competition, and the struggle to assert your beliefs. It symbolizes a battle for what you stand for, where differing opinions or opposing forces create tension and challenge. This card suggests that you're in a situation where your integrity is being tested, and you may need to defend your position or fight for what you believe in. The conflict may not be easy, but it's a necessary part of standing your ground and proving your commitment to your values. Embrace the challenge, knowing that it's through these struggles that you strengthen your resolve and clarify your true beliefs.

Reversed Meaning
The reversed Five of Wands indicates a desire to avoid conflict or a situation where tension and competition are beginning to subside. You may be seeking peace and resolution, opting to step back from arguments or power struggles that no longer serve you. This card can also suggest that the chaos and disagreements around you are lessening, allowing for clearer communication and collaboration. However, it can also warn of suppressed anger or unresolved issues that need to be addressed.

Six of Wands
Victory
The Six of Wands Tarot card signifies victory, recognition, and success. It represents a moment of triumph where your efforts are acknowledged and celebrated. This is not just a material victory but a spiritual one, where you've overcome challenges and emerged stronger and wiser. However, the card also serves as a reminder not to let success go to your head—remember those who supported you along the way. Acknowledging the contributions of others and staying humble in your achievements is key to maintaining harmony and continued success.

Reversed Meaning
The reversed Six of Wands suggests a lack of recognition or delayed success. You may feel overlooked or unappreciated for your efforts, leading to frustration or self-doubt. This card can also indicate a fall from grace or a setback after a period of success, where pride or overconfidence may have led to a downfall.

Seven of Wands
Testing your beliefs
The Seven of Wands Tarot card signifies a period of testing and defending your beliefs or positions. It represents a challenge where outside influences or competing viewpoints confront you, pushing you to stand firm in what you believe. This card encourages you to remain vigilant and not become complacent, as you may face obstacles that test your resolve. It's a reminder to assert yourself confidently and to be prepared to defend your stance, even when faced with opposition.

Reversed Meaning
The reversed Seven of Wands indicates a sense of being overwhelmed or feeling outmatched in the face of challenges. It suggests that you might be struggling to defend your beliefs or positions effectively, potentially leading to self-doubt or a retreat from confrontations. This card can also point to a lack of confidence or feeling like you're fighting an uphill battle without adequate support.

Eight of Wands
Ideas Fast & Furious
The Eight of Wands Tarot card represents rapid movement, swift progress, and an influx of ideas. It signifies a time when everything seems to be happening quickly, with your intuition and creative thoughts flowing freely. You may find yourself inundated with new ideas and opportunities, experiencing a burst of energy and momentum. This card encourages you to harness this fast-paced energy to take decisive action and capitalize on the opportunities presented. Embrace the flow of inspiration and stay agile, as things are moving fast, and your ability to adapt will be key to making the most of this dynamic period.

Reversed Meaning
The reversed Eight of Wands suggests delays, stagnation, or a lack of clarity in your endeavors. It indicates that progress may be slower than anticipated, with obstacles or miscommunications hindering your forward momentum. You might feel stuck or overwhelmed by too many ideas, leading to confusion or difficulty prioritizing. This card reversed can also signal that your intuitive insights or creative impulses are being blocked, making it challenging to take action or make decisions.

Nine of Wands
Spiritual Battle Won

The Nine of Wands Tarot card signifies a hard-fought victory and a sense of accomplishment after a spiritual or personal battle. It represents a period where you've faced significant challenges and obstacles, pushing yourself to your limits. Despite the hardships and exhaustion, you've managed to overcome these trials, emerging stronger and more resilient. This card acknowledges the effort and perseverance you've invested, celebrating your success in conquering the difficulties. While it's a time to take pride in your achievements, it also serves as a reminder to remain vigilant and prepare for any future challenges.

Reversed Meaning

The reversed Nine of Wands suggests feelings of burnout, vulnerability, or a lack of readiness to face new challenges. It may indicate that you are struggling with exhaustion or skepticism about your ability to continue pushing forward after a prolonged struggle. You might feel as if your efforts have been in vain, or that you're unable to fully recover from past battles.

Ten of Wands
Ask for Help

The Ten of Wands Tarot card highlights the burden of taking on too many responsibilities and the strain of carrying a heavy load. It signifies that you may be feeling overwhelmed by the sheer volume of tasks or obligations you've shouldered, leading to exhaustion and stress. This card underscores the importance of asking for help and delegating responsibilities to lighten your load. Recognize that you don't have to manage everything on your own; reaching out for support can relieve some of the pressure and help you regain a sense of balance and control.

Reversed Meaning

The reversed Ten of Wands indicates that you may be beginning to release or lighten your burdens, or it suggests that you're starting to see the end of a demanding phase. This card can point to a moment of relief from overwhelming responsibilities, where you're starting to delegate tasks more effectively or letting go of what no longer serves you. Alternatively, it may also reveal a tendency to procrastinate or avoid dealing with your obligations, leading to unresolved stress.

Page of Wands
Innovator
The Page of Wands represents a youthful energy of exploration, creativity, and innovation. This card embodies the spirit of an innovator, full of enthusiasm and a fresh perspective. It signifies the beginning of new projects or ideas, driven by a strong sense of curiosity and a desire to make things happen. The Page of Wands encourages you to embrace your creative impulses, take bold risks, and think "outside the box." It's a time to channel your innovative ideas into action and explore uncharted territories with excitement and optimism.

Reversed Meaning
The reversed Page of Wands suggests delays, lack of direction, or a setback in your creative or exploratory endeavors. It may indicate that you're experiencing doubts or a loss of enthusiasm for a new project or idea, possibly due to feeling overwhelmed or disheartened. This card can also point to a need for more focus or preparation before moving forward, as you might be struggling with Stagnant thinking or unrealistic expectations.

Knight of Wands
Questor
The Knight of Wands embodies the spirit of a questor adventurous, driven, and enthusiastic. This card represents a bold and dynamic energy, characterized by a relentless pursuit of goals and a passion for new experiences. It signifies a period of action and movement, where you're ready to take on challenges with confidence and courage. The Knight of Wands encourages you to embrace your inner explorer, to be daring in your pursuits, and to pursue your ambitions with determination and excitement. This is a time to follow your passions, fueled by your boundless enthusiasm and adventurous spirit.

Reversed Meaning
The reversed Knight of Wands suggests a lack of direction, impulsiveness, or scattered energy. It may indicate that you're struggling with a sense of aimlessness or difficulty committing to a course of action, often leading to frustration or a halt in progress. This card can also point to recklessness or an overzealous approach that results in burnout or conflicts.

Queen of Wands
Witch

The Queen of Wands embodies the essence of a powerful and charismatic witch—confident, vibrant, and dynamic. She exudes a magnetic energy, blending intuition with assertiveness to lead and inspire others. This card represents a strong sense of self, creativity, and leadership, showcasing someone who is both nurturing and fiercely independent. The Queen of Wands encourages you to embrace your inner strength, trust your instincts, and use your talents to create positive change. Her presence signifies a time to harness your creative potential, pursue your passions with determination.

Reversed Meaning

The reversed Queen of Wands indicates a period of self-doubt, insecurity, or a loss of confidence. You may be struggling to assert yourself or feeling overshadowed, leading to challenges in expressing your creativity or leadership. This card can also signal a need to reassess your approach, as you might be overextending yourself or struggling with burnout.

King of Wands
Shaman

The King of Wands embodies the archetype of the shaman—wise, visionary, and deeply connected to the spiritual realm. This card represents a figure of authority and leadership who combines charisma with profound insight, guiding others with a clear sense of purpose and a strong vision. The King of Wands is adept at using his intuitive wisdom and creative energy to inspire and lead, often serving as a catalyst for transformation and growth. He encourages you to harness your leadership qualities, trust your inner guidance, and take bold steps towards your goals.

Reversed Meaning

The reversed King of Wands suggests challenges with leadership, authority, or confidence. It may indicate that you're struggling with assertiveness, lacking direction, or experiencing difficulties in effectively leading or inspiring others. This card can also point to issues of impatience or a tendency to be domineering, leading to conflicts or strained relationships. It may be a sign that you need to reassess your approach, address any overconfidence or lack of focus, and reconnect with your inner strength.

Appendix: Glossary of Tarot Terms

Arcana
The two main sections of the Tarot deck: the Major Arcana (22 cards) and the Minor Arcana (56 cards). The Major Arcana cards represent significant life events or spiritual lessons, while the Minor Arcana cards focus on everyday experiences and situations.

Court Cards
The four face cards in each suit of the Minor Arcana: Page, Knight, Queen, and King. These cards often represent people, personality traits, or roles within a reading.

Interpretation
The act of analyzing and understanding the meanings of the cards in a reading. Interpretation can be influenced by card positions, combinations, and intuitive insights.

Intuition
The ability to understand or know something without the need for conscious reasoning. In Tarot, intuition helps readers interpret the cards beyond their traditional meanings.

Major Arcana
The 22 cards in the Tarot deck that represent major life themes, spiritual lessons, and archetypal energies. These cards include The Fool, The Magician, The High Priestess, and others.

Minor Arcana
The 56 cards in the Tarot deck divided into four suits: Pentacles, Cups, Swords, and Wands. These cards reflect everyday events and experiences and are often associated with specific aspects of life.

Querent
The person asking the question or seeking insight through a Tarot reading.

Reversed Cards
When a card appears upside down in a spread. Reversed cards can indicate blocked energies, challenges, or alternative meanings compared to their upright positions.

Reading
The process of interpreting the cards drawn in a spread to provide guidance, insight, or answers to a question.

Spread
A layout of cards drawn for a specific purpose or question. Common spreads include the three-card spread (past, present, outcome) and the Celtic Cross spread.

Signifier Card
A card selected to represent a person or situation in a reading. It is often chosen based on the querent's characteristics or the nature of the question. I usually look for this card on the bottom of the shuffle and consider it to be the last word, or summation of the reading.

Suits
The four categories within the Minor Arcana:
- **Pentacles:** Material aspects, finances, and career and health..
- **Cups:** Emotions, relationships, and creativity.
- **Swords:** Intellect, conflict, and decision-making.
- **Wands:** Action, inspiration, and personal growth.

Symbolism
The use of symbols within Tarot cards to convey deeper meanings and messages. Symbols can include imagery, colors, and patterns that provide insight into the card's interpretation.

Tarot Deck
A set of 78 cards used for divination, including the Major and Minor Arcana. Decks can vary in imagery and style but generally follow the same structure.

Tarot Journal
A personal journal used to record daily readings, reflections, and insights. Keeping a Tarot journal helps track progress and deepen understanding of the cards.
This glossary provides a quick reference to common Tarot terms and concepts, helping you navigate your Tarot journey with greater ease and understanding.

www.ingramcontent.com/pod-product-compliance
Lightning Source LLC
Chambersburg PA
CBHW071912070526
44583CB00016B/1952